The Physical Actor

The Physical Actor might well be titled "Actor as Dancer," so choreographically honed are its descriptions and analyses. At once manual and survey, the book is an engaging and inclusive overview of body techniques and their emotional connotations. In its specificity and precision, *The Physical Actor* is an essential resource for anyone who aspires to act or move.

Yvonne Rainer (choreographer)

Annie Loui's remarkable new book not only offers a unique step-by-step approach for integrating movement training with an actor's text, it also teaches actors how to live a deep moment-to-moment life with their scene partners physically. By clearly detailing a technique that connects impulse-driven contact improvisation with scene work in styles ranging from Shakespeare to Chekhov, Loui shows actors something new; how to listen with their bodies. An indispensable book.

Richard Brestoff (actor and author, *The Camera Smart Actor*)

Without Annie Loui, I would not have had the guts to work with Twyla Tharp. But I did. With no formal dance training, armed only with three years of movement education under Ms. Loui's guidance, I was cast as the lead of the Twyla Tharp/Bob Dylan musical *The Times, They Are A-Changin'*. Not unlike Twyla, Annie Loui understands that spatial awareness, partnering tools, an active imagination, and a courageous heart are all one needs to enhance her natural capacity to trust her instincts and, subsequently, create a vocabulary of movement that is deeply connected. This gem of a book is a must-have for actors who are searching for the right tools to unlock their body's full potential.

Jen Colella (actress)

Annie Loui is the real deal. I love her insights into the craft and her reminders of why we do this and why the physical work is important to the actor. Physical awareness is one of the elements of the craft that you must experience in order to recognize its importance and power in your work. When we watch artists who understand their bodies and physicality we are drawn to the story and that actor in particular. The physical actor completes the image, the story, the moment. While I am no longer a performer, I continue to use the training and awareness that I learned from working with Annie Loui every day.

Elliot Fox (managing director, Primary Stages)

Contents

Acknowledgments

Thanks to my parents, the theater director Wayne Loui and Professor Tuck Loui, for being shining examples, and always encouraging their children to create.

Thanks to my colleagues at UC Irvine for their congenial support especially Robert Cohen and Richard Brestoff for sage advice, friendly coffee, and careful reading. Large thanks are due to Talia Rodgers, my editor, who had faith.

And finally, thanks to my students over the years of practice in the studio. If you had not gone on the journey, this book would not exist.

Illustrative photos: Michael Lamont, Adrian Alita, and Sean Tarrant.

Practitioners: Annie Loui, Karin Hendricks, Evans Jarnefeldt, and Ethan Sawyer.

Additional contact improvisation photos: Adrian Alita and Sean Tarrant.

This manuscript was written in the library of the Ecole des Beaux Arts Rouen, France and in Silverado, California.

Introduction

What do we look for in a good actor? Engagement with the text, an understanding and passion about the ideas or point of view expressed; and an engagement with the "other" (whether actively onstage with him, or revealed in a monologue). We also demand that indefinable quality, a compelling "presence." All of these elements draw us in and compel us to live through the actor. Theater is a vicarious art form—we are all voyeurs experiencing emotion or ideas through a character's eyes—and we *want* to be drawn in, but it takes a forceful actor to bring us into his world. How do we create these "living" moments, and what can we do to elevate the actor's performance to this level of charged reality?

An alert, physical body is a conduit for emotional impulse, and the well-articulated and flexible body is capable of expressing nuance of emotion and "range" of being (from age to gender to psychological disposition). Michael Chekhov speaks of "radiating," Stanislavski refers to "projecting" and Robert Cohen speaks of "penetration." Ultimately, the actor relies on his physical instrument in voice and movement for this expression. A strong physical presence can be nurtured through exercises oriented toward relaxation within oneself, and a complete engagement with the objectives of the character.

Strong physical actors will be in a relaxed state of readiness, kinetically aware of the space they are in, the people they are around, and the imperceptible influences of motion and rhythm that surround them. Physical actors use all their senses, intuition, and intellect, to "inform" their physical being and actions on the stage without self-consciousness or over-intellectualizing.

I believe that every alert actor has the potential to develop these instincts, skills, and presence regardless of size, weight, or previous training, and this is achieved through a combination of physical and mental preparation and a bit of courage.

In this book, I will discuss theory and related studio exercises oriented toward the realization of our "uber"-actor. We will explore fundamentals of physical preparation in stretch, strength, and alignment; and the relationship of the actor to the physical environment, to the group, and to a specific "other." I have incorporated exercises over the years from different exemplary teachers of theater, dance, and martial arts, some of whom I have had the great good fortune to study with personally. Over my career working with actors onstage and in the classroom, I have tweaked these exercises toward my own specific goals. I believe this is called processing information and is the way in which I can bring my own very personal accumulation of knowledge and experience to the field. My training in Europe under the corporeal mime master Etienne Decroux and the Polish Tomaschevski mime/ballet master teacher Ella Jarosovitcz has greatly influenced my understanding of the usefulness of the articulated autonomous body. Work with dancer/choreographer Carolyn Carlson at the Paris Opera, and with the experimental theater director Jerzy Growtowski (as well as related studies in aikido and contact improvisation) has given my work in the theatrical physicality of mime a connection to sustained motion, instinct, and directed energy.

Mime trains the artist to structure physical images in space. There is always a resolution—even the most abstract work has a beginning, middle, and an end. By its very nature, mime organizes the body and mind in tandem to communicate, because in most cases the mime is both the performer and playwright, and the director/choreographer. The young actor practicing mime also learns to connect impulse and emotion with gesture—even the smallest rotation or inclination of the head, chest, or pelvis, realigns emotional impact in the audience's eye. Every movement counts. Accuracy of the motion informed by intention (I turn my head to see what made the noise, and my chest rises in anticipation of drawing closer to my destination) makes the actor compelling. So we gain accuracy of hand/eye motor control, connection of idea or emotion to gesture, and a certain physical and intellectual self-reliance through mime. But for its many positive aspects, traditional mime imposes a rigidity and stylization on the body that does not always translate directly to the naturalistic contemporary stage.

So we temper mimetic control with the fluid spontaneity of "contact improvisation." A dance improvisation form developed in the 1970s by modern dancer, choreographer, aikido practitioner Steve Paxton, contact improvisation is defined as a partnering form that consists of an energy and weight exchange between two people. Contact emphasizes alert physical "listening," complicity of weight, and instinctive responses. Basic tumbling, energy exchange exercises, and partnering dance lifts are its fundamental building blocks. A good contact practitioner develops an alertness to physical nuance, an ability to follow through a line of motion, and an unconscious kinetic attentiveness to the "other" that is deeply attractive to the voyeuristic audience. Contact improvisation in the acting studio translates directly to scene work, and the impulses developed for acrobatic and dance-like expressions of contact transform into a physically charged realism incorporating text.

In order to arrive at our goal of the compelling, capable, physical actor, we first look at the actor's body, developing it through daily warm-up into a strong, flexible, and aligned instrument (Chapter 1). Physical awareness of self in space, and self within a group is honed through exercises in spatial awareness (Chapter 2) and mime studies promote fine motor control and a certain physical–intellectual connection

(Chapter 3). Partnering skills (Chapter 4) develop physical receptivity, heighten co-ordination and sustained motion, and create an active physical responsiveness to the "other." Culminating this exploration, our actor goes to the theatrical stage, incorporating text with the instinctive responsiveness and compelling presence of contact improvisation (Chapter 5). While absorbing the physical techniques outlined in this book, we simultaneously turn toward the creation of original performance (Chapter 6), promoting an intelligent imagination that allows the actor to process technique and make it their own.

Welcome. It's time to work.

CHAPTER 1

Warm-up and Alignment

Warm-up: what we do and how we approach it

There are many ways to nirvana; and a variety of dance and martial art forms can be used for a satisfactory warm-up. However, some basic movement guidelines must be followed in structuring and practicing a warm-up for actor preparedness.

1   *Begin with a simple aerobic sequence for cardio-vascular engagement*   I often begin a warm-up with three minutes of concentrated aerobic dancing; or we run the Mao Sequence (a five-minute comprehensive series of calisthenic/martial arts movements developed by Chairman Mao's advisors to the public health). Of primary importance here is getting a circulation of blood flow to facilitate muscular stretch in the subsequent floor exercises.

2   *Stretch and strength exercises should both be covered*   They are mutually beneficial—once flexibility is improved, the support-ing muscular structure must be strengthened, particularly the lower back and abdomen. Stretches must be done in a way to facilitate improvement for even the most inflexible of actors:

slow extended breath with movement is useful; basic yoga stretches are optimum.

3   *Proper alignment* This refers to alignment of the spine and shoulders, pelvis, knees and feet and should be addressed within the warm-up exercises. Alexander technique, Pilates, Feldenkrais, to name a few, all address proper placement of the body over the feet to best facilitate easeful motion. In the course of the notated warm-up and the introduction of mime isolations (in Chapter 3), I will touch on a few alignment exercises I have found useful.

4   *Repetition* I had a new student respectfully address me after two weeks of class saying that he wanted to do a new warm-up—he already knew our exercises. I told him that I thought Baryshnikov probably already knew how to plié, but I suspect that he still did them every day. A daily warm-up is precisely that—a series of exercises repeated for the cumulative beneficial results. Repetition with small variations is useful in developing stretch, strength, and control. The sequence should basically remain consistent with small variations to keep the practitioner mentally alert.

5   *Working intelligently* Of equal importance, and often overlooked, is the need for the actor to understand what he/she is working for in each exercise, and where to work from. For example, extending the torso out over the legs to stretch the hamstrings is a movement that needs to be initiated from the lower back. Whether you are perfect in execution today is immaterial—that you work intelligently and within your own physical limitations is imperative. "Burn" and sharp pain are not good—a long stretch initiated correctly, relaxing everything that is not needed in that particular movement, tends to be productive.

6   *Imagery* This is one of the most valuable tools for the physical actor—and warm-up exercises can be engaged in most productively by the actor if specific images are connected to

the movements. This can be done with the most literal of approaches ("imagine that you are a marionette with a string attached to the top of your head, elongating your spine, and pulling you up"). For the neophyte this will probably be effective as a first attempt to connect imagery with movement; however, I find subtle suggestions most useful ("the neck is long, and the shoulders wide"). The neck may not be long, nor the shoulders wide, but the suggestion is now there—the actor should not use this as a command to make the neck long, but rather let the suggestion inform movement. I find that the actor's body that is physically alert and fit will respond almost unconsciously to such suggestions with subtle and effective adjustments.

7   *Respect* Aim to respect yourself as a serious training professional, respect the workspace, respect the person conducting the warm-up, and respect your colleagues; these are all modalities to be encouraged. Integrity of self within the work allows you to approach it in a relaxed and simultaneously energized state of being. The external discipline of engaging in rote exercise is useful, but only up to point. One engages consciously in the exercises, actively working on the specific task at hand. As an actor/practitioner you need to take responsibility for yourself, and to actively embrace the work, respecting yourself in the daily practice of your chosen profession.

HASTE

I am running from the busy subway through the evening streets by the Gare du Nord. I am late again for my beginning aikido class, and almost knock over a solitary man loitering in the doorway, elegantly dressed in a three-piece suit and smoking a cigarette. I pause, startled, and my dance clothes, aikido clothes, and left-over peanut butter sandwich fall out of my bag. The man graciously steps back, "Ah, excuse me Mademoiselle," and hands me my scattered belongings. I look up from the ground as I thank him. The man in the suit is my aikido sensei, Maître Noro. "Oh, Monsieur, excusez-moi,"

I am flustered trying to articulate excuses for my lateness (the subway, the dance class that got out late), chagrined at having charged into the master teacher in this world of martial arts where hierarchy and respect are critical. He waves excuses away, "Entrez, mademoiselle." I run down the stairs to the dressing room, throwing off my street clothes and throwing on my aikido gi—mandatory white trouser and jacket for the martial arts beginner—and race back upstairs to the dojo. Instead of the normal beginners teacher, standing at the door of the dojo is Maître Noro himself, this time impeccably dressed in the aikido hakama, joking with another black belt. He looks like he has been standing there forever. He turns and smiles at me in recognition, "Ah, mademoiselle" and with a little bow, welcomes me into the dojo. I enter, the door closes, and we bow to the picture of the founder of Aikido. Maître Noro demonstrates the partnering work we are about to do and we bow to him. We find a partner and bow to each other. And we begin.

The warm-up that I do utilizes exercises taken primarily from aikido, yoga, modern dance, and mime. There are many variations on these exercises that can also be useful. However, the general sequence should not be changed; stretches of upper back alternate with reverse stretches of the lower back, and the order is purposeful.

Noted below is my daily warm-up with some guiding suggestions. Advanced warm-up usually includes a ballet floor barre (not included in this sequence). Most of these exercises are repeated three times. "Extra" denotes additional stretch movements that are usually only executed during the first repetition. Alternate "Variations" are also indicated, as are "segues" to move seamlessly from one exercise to the next. A chiropractor once told me that many of my warm-up exercises were the same he gave to patients for rehabilitation.

Warm-up sequence

The cat

Begin by resting your forehead on your hands and elongating your neck so that the weight of the forehead presses straight down into the ground. Note the length of your spine, and the released and yet energized extension of your body against the floor. It is imperative to begin a stretch sequence in this relaxed but viscerally "ready" state. Give yourself a little minute here, particularly on days when you are having a little difficulty focusing.

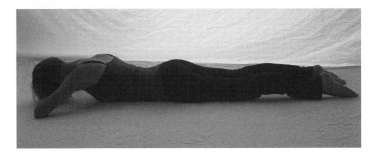

Bring your hands comfortably by your shoulders and scoop up sequentially, forehead, nose, chin until you are arched back in the yoga cobra position. Push your shoulders down, and feel the stretch from your pelvic bone to your chin.

Move back into the crouch, releasing your pelvis back onto your heels, and allowing your arms to stretch forward in opposition.

Extra: walk your fingers forward, leave them there and release your elbows to the ground. You will feel the extra stretch through your shoulders.

Come up on all fours, curl your toes under, and lift your coccyx (tailbone) into the air making your body into a perfect triangle (the yoga downward facing dog).

Focus on pushing your lower back down and flattening it out, and simultaneously pressing your heels into the ground.

> *Extra: alternate pressing your heels down to the ground, bending one knee and then the other, stretching out the calf of the straight leg.*

Release your pelvis down to the ground, sliding back into the cobra arch.

Release all the way down to the ground.

Repeat three times.

Segue: at the end of the last repetition, stretch out your arms, and roll over onto your back.

The bridge

Bend your knees and grab a hold of your ankles.

Your neck is long, your shoulders are wide, and your lower back is positioned firmly against the ground. If you have problems comfortably holding onto your ankles in this position, let go of the ankles and keep the approximate shape, concentrating on the elongation of your spine.

Extra: contract your lower abdominal muscles (imagine taking your navel down to your spine), and tilt your pelvis up about an inch off of the floor. Hold that for a count of three, and then release it down. Repeat three times.

Repeating that same motion, scoop your tailbone out and up, peeling your vertebrae one by one off the ground until your pelvis is at maximum extension toward the ceiling.

Imagine leaving the pelvis at maximum extension as you lower the vertebrae one by one to the ground, and end by releasing the pelvis last.

Repeat three times.

Focus on separating the vertebrae as much as possible when you peel them up off the ground, and then lower them back down.

Segue: let go of your ankles and entwine your fingers, pushing your palms up toward the ceiling. Your shoulders will get a luxurious stretch as they are pulled off the ground.

Neck stretch

Place your hands behind your head, and using only your arms, lift your heavy head toward your chest. The knees are still bent. Now turn your head gently from one side to the other, allowing its full weight to lie in your hands. Imagine strings attached to your elbows, pulling your arms forward (remember a relaxed neck and head weigh 10 pounds/4.5kg).

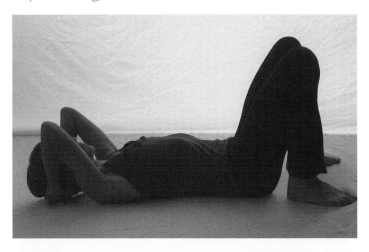

Now release it.

You can also work your lower abdominal connection here at the same time—focus on the navel reaching back for the spine and the tailbone tilting slightly up as you stretch your neck and head forward.

Segue: imagine someone pulling forward on your elbows even harder, pulling you up to sitting.

The butterfly

Bring your feet in toward your pelvis and allow your knees to fall open to the sides.

Extra: press one knee down into the ground, placing pressure slightly above the knee and to the outside of the knee for optimum stretch. This is a simple muscle reminder to your knee and hip that they can open up this far. Now press the other knee to the ground.

Take a hold of your feet (probably squashing your fingers) and straighten your back, imagining the connection from the top of your head through your spine down into your coccyx. Pulse your knees in tiny butterfly flaps. As you pull your shoulders down, your spine lengthens out.

Extend the legs forward as you extend the arms up.

Extending from the lower back, stretch out over your legs, imagining your chest on your knees.

Reach out with arms and scoop back up to sitting, and then release the arms down to the sides.

Hold on to your feet and bring them in toward your pelvis, knees falling out to the sides, spine released back in a curve.

Undulate back up to your original butterfly position (starting with the lower back undulate all the way through the spine, ending with the head).

Repeat three times.

Variations: stretch out over one leg at a time, centering your chest on that knee. Then stretch out over the other leg.

Stretch over legs with flexed feet.

Segue: on the final repetition, scoop out and up to sitting, drop the arms and experiment raising, dropping, and rolling the shoulders, noting that the back remains straight and strong and unaffected by the shoulder motion.

Extra: side bend. Sitting perfectly straight, sweep your right arm up to the side and above your head and then continue the motion, leaning over to the left side while anchoring your right hip down to the ground (it would like to come off the ground here—don't let it). Slide your left arm out to support your weight in this sideways lean. You want to think of two things here: sliding

out, reaching with the arm as far as you can to the side (imagine your thumb behind your head as you bend—this image can keep you from tilting forward); and simultaneously counterbalancing the stretch with your right hip fixed firmly on the ground. Come back up to sitting, and bend now to the other side.

Segue: entwine the fingers and push the palms to the ceiling reminding yourself of the perfect connection between your coccyx and the top of your head. Now pushing those arms forward, counterbalance yourself down to the ground, lowering vertebrae by vertebrae.

The plough

Lie flat on your back, bend your knees and kick your legs behind your head, toes touching the ground (you might need to support your back with your hands in this position, and that is fine).

Extra: straighten one leg back behind you and bend the opposite knee and allow it to touch the ground. Then alternate.

Allow both knees to bend, touching the ground on either side of your head (or as close to the ground as you can comfortably release).

Imagine a scorpion's tail—a flexible curve from the pelvis to the neck. Remember to breathe here. Your head will not break off, you will not suffocate, and your relaxed neck and upper back will allow your knees to get closer to the ground with each breath out.

Straighten both legs behind your head, pushing your heels back into the ground for one last stretch.

Roll back vertebrae by vertebrae controlling the unraveling of your spine by imagining someone pulling back on your flexed feet, gradually allowing each vertebrae to gently roll down to the ground.

Your pelvis is now on the ground and your legs are extended straight up in the air. Point your toes as hard as you can.

Release at the knees. Now release your feet down to the ground, and then slide them all the way out until you are lying flat against the ground.

Variation: take hold of your flexed feet with your hands and hold on to them as long as you can, guiding the gradual unrolling of your spine until your pelvis is back on the ground.

Sternum lift

Lying comfortably on your back, stretch your arms out to the sides and slightly up toward your head (imagine them as wings). In this position, imagine your lower back down toward the ground, and then imagine flattening your ribcage (this will further elongate your spine).

Push off your arms, and leading with your chest, come all the way up to sitting. Imagine your breast bone (sternum) leading the movement arching up off the ground, supported effortlessly by your "wings" propelling you up to sitting.

Point your toes and bend your knees, letting them fall out to the sides as you bring your arms into a circle in front of you while curving your back. Imagine a beach ball in your circled arms as you counterbalance leaning back in a beach ball-shaped curve.

Straighten the legs, scooping forward with the arms up to a straight back, arms above the head.

Release down to the ground, counterbalancing with your arms in front of you.

Repeat three times.

Segue: on the third repetition after the scoop forward, let your knees bend (this time in front of your body), and hold on to them with your arms, release back into a curved spine.

Spine undulation

Slowly undulate up the spine on slow count of four, starting with the lower back and progressing up through the middle back, upper back, shoulders, and head to a fully elongated sitting.

Imagine a line running from your coccyx up through the spine and off the top of your head.

Release back into a full curve, beginning again with the lower back and ending with the head.

On the third repetition, after undulating up, let go of your knees, and extend your arms up on that line, pulling your shoulders down as you reach toward the sky.

Open your arms out to the sides, and imagine pushing down the air as your back remains perfectly long and straight.

Close your arms in front of you, holding on to your knees again and extending your spine up higher just a fraction more.

Segue: release all the way down to the floor.

Floating

Close in your ribcage again, and press your lower back down toward the ground.

Rise up! Arms and legs are in the air as you improvise floating in outer space, raising and lowering your torso and legs without hands or feet touching the ground.

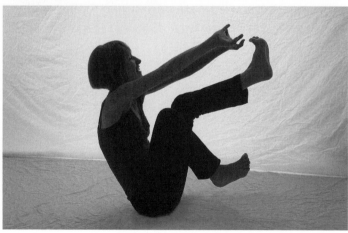

Lower all the way down.

Come back up! And this time imagine an alternate substance to "float" in (the Mediterranean Sea?, cherry jello?, snowflakes?), and release back down.

Repeat this abdomen exercise three times.

Extra (advanced): come up to a curled, floating position holding on to your knees or feet, but, of course, not touching the ground.

Extend your legs straight as high as you can; and then extend your back—imagine pulling up out of the lower abdomen to make your body into a perfect triangle.

Arms are open to the sides, palms to the ceiling, as you imagine your chest open to the ceiling. Hold this for a count of eight, always pulling up out of your lower abdominal muscles.

Release back to the curled floating postion.

Repeat one or two more times and then release all the way to the ground.

Fast abs

Come back up! (Feet off the ground, knees bent, arms around knees, but this time hands clapping in front of the knees.)

Go back down! (Counterbalancing torso and legs, arms gently slapping the ground above the head.)

The moment the feet and hands hit the ground, rise back up again clapping hands in front of knees.

Repeat fifteen to twenty-five times as fast as you can, keeping the simultaneous co-ordination of arms and legs.

As you come up each time, imagine the motion originating from your lower abs. You may find that you need a little padding (sweat pants or a mat) in the first few weeks while your body learns to quickly lower without slamming vertebrae into the ground.

Realign against the floor

Bring your knees into your chest and feel your lower back comfortably elongated against the ground.

Make little circles with your knees pulling slightly closer to your body and circling to the side, and away, and to the other side, allowing the gentle pressure to travel in your back. Now circle in the other direction. Alternate directions and pressure as you wish.

Make very small, almost imperceptible circles, and feel the subtle responses in the musculature of your back (the homeopathic medicine of the spine).

Spine twist

Take your left knee into your chest (the right leg remains comfortably elongated against the ground).

With the right arm, pull the left knee gently across your body and all the way down to the ground.

Leave the left arm on the ground, and relax into this luxurious twist, concentrating on the left knee and left shoulder releasing in perfect opposition. Breathe here, allowing the stretch to deepen with each breath out.

Slowly trace a circle on the ground using your left arm, and, like the hands of a clock, sweep that arm above your head and then continue circling (meeting up with your prone right arm), sweeping across your body and finally opening out into the original position. Try to follow the action of the "minute hand" with your eyes and head (this will encourage your upper body to stretch out and conversely release in, as the arm circles).

Repeat this slow, continuous circle twice more, and then roll onto your back, bringing both knees into the chest.

Let the left leg down and straighten out, and this time the right knee is gently pulled across the body and down to the ground on the left-hand side. Opening your arms out to the sides, comfortably twisted, repeat the sequence on the right side. End by pulling both knees gently into the chest.

Segue: release your hands, and leaving your knees bent, let your feet drop down to the ground. Note the relaxed elongation of your back against the ground.

Slide your legs out straight, reminding yourself that your lower back remains down toward the ground as your ribcage flattens, while your neck is long and your shoulders wide.

Breathe here, relaxed and energized, and ready to work.

CHAPTER 2

Space

Sitting at a café with a mirrored wall, I notice the reflections of other people sitting around me engaged in solitary café activity (reading the newspaper, smoking, drinking coffee). I see that small shifts of action from one person (taking a pen out of a purse, for instance) trigger small unconscious bursts of action from neighboring tables (a sneeze at table one creates a rubbing of the eye at table two, which triggers a final sip of coffee at table three). We all influence each other constantly in subtle and unconscious ways.

The great twentieth-century humanitarian and scientist Buckminster Fuller speaks of intuition as information whose source is the hundreds of unconsciously processed perceptions we receive every day. The slight waft of air by my right shoulder means that someone is passing close behind me, so I pivot to the left to avoid potential collision. What I say is that I have "intuited" their presence—what I have actually done is to use my senses to gain tactical information about negotiating the space, and then responded accordingly. There is no time for conscious thought. A large part of the physical actor's work with space has to do with an ability to play back and forth between sense perception/intuition and a conscious engagement with the actor's objective.

The well-trained actor moves freely through space with assurance and respect for objects and people. This actor is at ease within the architecture of the set, moving with a subtle awareness of their relationship with physical place as well as their relationship with other actors. This actor is also preternaturally alert to kinetic indications of shift of intention in others, and responds to their changes without conscious thought. Movement dialogues develop ranging from overt responses (my raised hand signals the waiter to come) to small visceral reactions in a Chekhov play (when Helena puts down her teacup, the doctor crosses his leg and her husband turns the page of a book). Every action has a reaction. This law of physics also applies to human behavior.

We are all constantly living in a material, physical world composed of endless variety and nuance of sound, motion, and rhythm—the implicit rhythms present as the wind blows through tree branches in autumn and leaves fall from the tree is not only poetic, it is also an explicit example of the richness to be perceived in natural relationships. As "human animals" we utilize our honed instincts, intuitively relating to other people, places, and objects. In doing so we become alert, relaxed, and effortlessly co-ordinated within our own bodies, and within the group dynamic.

Spatial exercises

Milling exercises (the random patterns of a group in motion) are used often in our group warm-up, and are a natural extension of walking with an awareness of the self in space, the self within the group, and the self in direct relationship with one other person.

Milling exercise 1

Begin by walking freely at a good continuous pace through the space (*not* in a prescribed pattern). Explore the perimeters of the space, actively making eye contact with everyone you pass by.

Do the same moving backward. You discover that in order to walk backward and negotiate the space without bumping into other people, you need to make small half-turns. As you confront other people doing the same thing, do not stop to avoid their trajectory through space, particularly do not stop or slow down if it looks like you are going to collide; rather, pivot to avoid collision, and continue. It takes only a small rotation of the body to become a narrow "target" for collision.

Mill moving forward again.

This exercise can be repeated as often as seems productive to engender freedom of motion through space and kinetic group awareness.

At this point in time, the group should be physically warmed-up, perceptively alert, and able to move between forward and backward motions without too much anxiety or conscious negotiation of the space.

Milling exercise 2

Continue milling easily through the space making eye contact with everyone you see, moving forward and backward with turns at will, easily relating to the group.

Shift into a relationship with one person—the structure for the physical interaction is the same, simple walking at a good pace. You may end up walking side by side, or moving away or toward the other person, circling them, or walking behind them, or many, many other combinations and variations of physical floor patterns in relationship to one other person. These interactions are seamless, unconstructed, playful, and alert (like any good conversation).

Move back into the group milling. All this time you have also remained alert to the group and the perimeters of the space, avoiding collision, remaining kinetically respectful, and keeping pace.

Seamlessly shift into a relationship with a new partner. Sometimes you will find that you are working in a trio or that your partner is unaware of your "partnership." Relax, stay vigilant and playful, and continue doing your work in awareness and reaction. Trios are more complex, but demand the same attentiveness as a normal partnering. "Ghost partners" can be enjoyable—they always catch on eventually.

After several shifts of partner and release back into the general group milling, you will be able to automatically shift partners when the relationship is over. It may endure for only a few quick side by side steps before one of you is engaged with a new relationship, or it may develop into a lengthier exploration of mutual energies within the space. However, these relationships are meant to change, and your goal is to continue to work within the group, letting the continually shifting patterns of motion and individuals take you along with them.

Milling exercise 3

You will start the milling exercise as before, but this time you will be using music to establish a common walking rhythm.

Begin by playing music that has a steady and easily discernible beat (World Music is a good source for "milling music") and clap along with the beat. When the group is in unison, walk in time to the beat (one step for every beat). Move through the space, again milling in relationship to the group, to the perimeters of the room, and to individual partners but this time walking and turning to the established beat.

After a few minutes of exploring milling with this externally dictated rhythm, stop and clap the music in half-time. Now travel through the space, milling in half-time (one step for every two beats).

Repeat the same sequence of instruction in double-time (two steps for every beat). This is obviously harder because the pace is fast and must remain consistent, so you must quickly become alert and actively engaged as the pace accelerates.

Introduce "stopping" as a final option within the milling exercise.

After exploring these different rates of motion, freely mill using all the options of rhythm while physically relating to other members of the group. At this point in time you should be able to switch partners with ease and enjoy relating to each other in differing rhythms. It is important to simply walk and turn with the beat, and not embellish your movement with dance steps (which is a seductive possibility when asked to improvise with music).

Good milling is like driving: you keep your eye on the car in front of you, but you also use your peripheral vision to stay alert to the cars around you. Half-turns replace rear-view mirrors. Navigation is done continuously, effortlessly, with no excessive intellectualization or reckoning. Experience and basic driving skills help us respond easily to the ever-changing flow of traffic. Milling exercises can be repeated often, and for varying lengths of time. As actors become more adept, lengthier milling sessions (somewhere beyond a mild fatigue or boredom) can engender a "floating" sensation, where actors are conscious of participating in an effortless group energy, flowing from one relationship to another at a consistent group pace, with endless variety, co-ordination, and control.

I often use milling exercises as part of the warm-up for a contact improvisation session.

ABOUT WORKING WITH MUSIC

Twentieth-century physical theater and mime masters Jean Dorcy, Etienne Decroux, and Ella Jarosivitcz have all engaged in the thorny debate about the difference between dance and mime. After all these are both art forms that demand expressiveness through the medium of the physical body in space. Interestingly, all three experts agreed that the essential difference lies in the use of music: for the dancer music dictates the movement, and for the mime an internal rhythm must motivate action.

In our case we want it all. The strong physical actor should also have a good grounding in basic dance forms, which are almost inevitably dictated by music. Improved co-ordination, a sense of lyricism, and the complicity of unison movement are only some of the benefits derived from dancing to an externally dictated rhythm in prescribed dance styles. However, the physical actor is a theatrical being, and his/her movements are generated by a complex of internal emotional rhythms, kinetic responses to scene partners, and by the content and rhythm of the text. The following exercise falls into the former category, and can be executed with either a steady verbal rhythm or using music as a guide.

Passing diagonals

Stand across the room from your partner (no diagonals yet). A steady medium-slow beat is established. Starting on your right foot, walk across the room toward your partner in five steps, one step for each count. At this point you should both have reached the middle of the room and be directly facing each other almost nose to nose. On the sixth count, pivot on your right foot to pass your partner, with a half-turn clockwise stepping back on your left. You have now taken their place, and the two of you are facing one another. Walk backward continuously facing your partner for six steps. You have now completed the entire approach and retreat and are ready to begin again, starting on your right foot.

Once the mechanics of distance are negotiated and the half-turn clockwise is established (easily done when both partners are pivoting on the right foot to pass and stepping back on the left to face each other), you are ready to "take the space" moving confidently in full steps of equal size forward and backward. An easy verbal command to facilitate this sequence is:

Forward: "And 1, 2, 3, 4, 5, and 6" (passing on the "and 6").

Backward: "And back, 2, 3, 4, 5, again" (moving away from each other, and ready to start up again).

Pick up the pace, establishing a faster count either verbally or with music.

A certain freedom and excitement is engendered with this continuous movement, potential collision (easefully avoided with a pivot), and equally easeful retreat. Through repetition, partners develop a complicit sense of tension and release in their mutual flow of energy forward, almost colliding, and then confidently ricocheting away like two repelling magnets of equal force.

Change positions in space using the four corners of the room, so that partners are now approaching each other from separate diagonals (here are those diagonals). With a group of twelve actors you will have six pairs, three actors in each of the four corners. Now run the exercise alternating diagonals. Once one pair has completed the full approach and retreat, begin again using a pair from the opposite diagonal.

Continue alternating diagonals, and when the group is comfortable with this new spatial alignment, overlap diagonals starting the second couple forward when the first couple is in retreat, on the "and back."

Now the stakes are higher, and there is less margin for error as the actors are asked to move accurately through space on the count, avoiding potential collision with ease, and moving backward to create an empty space that the next couple is already moving forward to fill. Overlapping demands attentiveness: the smaller the group, the more often you will be called on to move. In diagonal groups I often ask the waiting partners to take care of the person backing up (guiding them away from walls, and other potential obstacles).

Amoeba exercise: "instant art"

One person in the group takes a position in space, and one by one the rest of the group add to the original configuration, positioning themselves in response to whatever shape is already constructed. You should avoid putting weight on anyone, but you do want to be in close physical proximity. By the time the entire group is participating, you will see that a construction has organically evolved —usually aesthetically engaging with varying shapes, directions of energy, and levels.

On a verbal command, the "amoeba" moves for a slow count of four, and then freezes for a count of four. The initiation of motion comes from the line of energy and weight already established by your position, simultaneously influenced by the action of the rest of the group. Working like a good single-celled organism, you focus on complicity of action, while not losing your own individual trajectory.

After a few repetitions of freezes and motion, two factors emerge. The first is a realization that moving at a unified speed with a consistent rate of motion helps to establish harmonious group action. (Group flow is interrupted if one person moves much faster or varies the rate of motion within the four count.) The second is that the freezes become wonderfully dynamic, reminiscent of baroque statuary groups. There is implied emotion within the many different lines of motion and changing dynamics and interactions. In a typical amoeba, you might see a freeze with three actors facing the same direction, one holding onto the shoulders of the other two to brace themselves. Next to them another actor is turned away leaning into the chest of their partner, and two others kneel in front of them with their arms extended to the sky but heads turned to face the trio. There is an unconscious sensitivity to group construction, proximity to other actors, and use of positive and negative space in shape and positioning. When this exercise is repeated with actors honestly following through the physical line of action implied in their last position while responding to the group flow, the action becomes effortless for the practitioner and the freeze is an unplanned, harmonious image—"instant art." The unexpected, and almost choreographed, tableaux that can emerge are compelling in their power and kaleidoscopic transformation.

This exercise is valuable for finding individual motion within a group dynamic. It can also be used as a choreographic tool when combined with specific imagery.

PERCEPTION

Jerry Letvin, a noted neuro-biologist at Columbia University, tells about his research at MIT in the late 1970s concerning visual perception and frogs' eyes. Frogs normally have "selective" vision—the world to them is a haze of indistinct objects with two exceptions: other frogs and food. But put in a position of danger, they suddenly develop a heightened awareness, and can see everything in their surroundings very clearly (rocks, water, trees, and the enemy, as well as other frogs and food).

We have to ask ourselves if we bear a certain resemblance to these lazy frogs—always physically capable of seeing, but only fully functioning when pushed to alertness. The following exercises are used to heighten peripheral vision and alertness and to promote quick physical responses.

Fishes exercise

This exercise follows the swimming patterns of a school of fish.

One member of the group (Alicia for example) is the leader (Head Fish). All others crowd around the Head Fish trying to be as close to her as possible without actually touching. You can position yourself in front, behind, or on either side of the Head Fish.

The Head Fish is free to move anywhere in space that she chooses, and the objective of every member of the group is to always stay as close to her as possible, no matter where she goes or how fast she travels. You must always face the same direction as the Head Fish, no matter how abruptly she changes direction. You will find that sudden turns will throw the entire group into new configurations —the person who was behind the leader is now in front as the Head Fish reverses direction. Stay determined, follow relentlessly. Whenever she wants, the Head Fish can stop moving, and this signifies the end of her term as Head Fish.

At this point in time, everyone in the group has the option to change their position within the group, or to rest in place (move down to the floor). But you need to stay alert, because a new Head Fish (self-chosen) will emerge in this temporary stillness, and you will be obliged to follow this new leader.

Trust/nod exercise 1

The group begins in a large circle. Your objective is to walk to someone else's place in the circle; however, you may only move there when you are given permission by that person. Permission is shown by a nod "yes" of the head. When this agreeable colleague nods, you have your cue to begin walking to take their place.

But before you arrive, *they* need to vacate, looking quickly for "permission" to take someone else's place in the circle.

And so the exercise is set in motion: as soon as someone has given permission, they need to look for permission from a third person, creating a chain of interdependent movements as people take on new "homes" in the circle. The same rules apply to everyone: before vacating your position, you need to get "the permission nod" from an alert colleague. Alert, because the only way that you signal your need for a new place to go is by intently looking at the assembled group, scanning for that nod of permission. As a member of the circle, anyone is eligible to participate, but only those members of the group who remain vigilant to the need of their colleagues will play.

You will find that the best way to know who needs a nod, is to follow the action as it unfolds. You will soon find that walking purposefully and steadily to your new "home" helps the rest of the circle to understand who needs to vacate and is in need of a permission nod in order to move. If your colleague is not able to find a new home before you arrive, the exercise stops, and restarts with a renewed commitment from the group to stay alert to each other.

There is no specific person responsible for the exercise not working. It is group responsibility to stay alert to individual need, and individual responsibility to focus intently when scanning the group for the nod. Sometimes you will find that more than one person nods—in this case just choose which nod to accept and make your choice clear by moving directly to your new home. Avoid the urge to "help" your colleague by moving more slowly if they have not vacated in time. Also avoid the urge to broadcast your need by unnecessary gesticulating—your focused intention should be enough to get their attention. (You will also find that narrowing focus to one individual creates a specific intensity that is hard to miss.)

After several rounds you will find that the actors respond more quickly, having learned that vigilant attentiveness to the action makes them more successful participants. This is a lovely exercise for engendering complicity within a group—we all want to win, and in order to achieve the goal one must "listen" hard, respond positively and immediately, and then look to the group for equal engagement in the moment.

Trust/nod exercise 2

We now take alertness and responsiveness to a heightened level by raising the stakes. Just as one would make an acting scene more vital and compelling by creating urgency in the actor's motivation, we make the physical need to find permission and move before the new "tenant" gets there even more urgent by picking up the pace. When group complicity is established and the pace is steady with few stops and re-starts, the exercise leader can pick up the pace to a slow trot.

You will notice that things happen a lot faster now—permission must be granted and then looked for very quickly. Unexpectedly with the increased speed, the skill level improves. The faster the pace, the higher the stakes, and the more alert, complicit, and responsive the actors become.

After successfully operating at this pace, increase the speed to a full-out run. At this point you will feel as if you are participating in a sports event—a sense of team spirit develops as each actor strains to follow the unpredictable escalating group action, and is ready to run when needed.

READINESS

Polish experimental theater master Jerzy Grotowski had a lot to say about this sense of "readiness," and how it relates to theater. My experience working with him in France during an intensive workshop on "instinctive movement" readily demonstrates his beliefs. After acceptance to the Grotowski workshop held in a twelfth-century abbey in Brittany, a train ticket was mailed to my home in Paris. With the ticket were written instructions to walk from the train station to a certain nearby house, and wait there for a van that would transport me to the workshop location deep in the French countryside. I was thrilled and nervous about working with this great master, and a little uneasy about this mysterious communication. And so, on the day of travel, I was reassured to see several other people get off the train, directions in hand, and walk toward the same house carrying the same recommended workshop gear. We were welcomed at the door, and told that the van would soon arrive, and we should be prepared to go as soon as it came; meanwhile we should make ourselves at home. This was early afternoon. As we made cups of tea in the kitchen and quietly waited, suitcases in hand (there were six of us total—all strangers), we discovered four other people playing cards on the second floor. They too were waiting for the van, and had been there since late morning. In the general sense of anticipation, uncomfortable silence shifted to occasional conversations which dwindled back to silence. As afternoon turned to evening, there was a noise at the door, and all heads turned as three more people arrived holding the same piece of paper with the same instructions. They were also told by the workshop coordinator that the van would arrive soon, so be prepared to go at any moment. The van finally arrived at 10pm with no apologies and no explanation, and took us to our workshop destination in the dark. I only realized later that this first "wasted" day was actually the first day of the workshop. During this entire period of waiting, and waiting to begin a workshop we were all anxiously anticipating, I noticed a kind of preter-natural attentiveness in myself to any sound at the door or in the street. I was alert (and bored, and fatigued and uneasy), and when the van finally came and delivered us to the abbey grounds, we were immediately plunged into a physically demanding relentless four-hour work session running through the night woods. There was no time for pre-conceived ideas about dance or movement, and no time to process the unjustness of the nine-hour wait— there was only the option to respond without thought using every instinct available on the unknown terrain in the dark. I was learning an important lesson about readiness, and this, in fact, was the core lesson of Grotowski's theater workshop on instinctive movement—always be alert and ready to work. Always be alive to possibility. The call can come at any time, and you need to be in a relaxed state of readiness.

Environment/group exercise

This is a seductively simple exercise taken from Grotowski's work on instinctive movement. It is actually very difficult to execute honestly. Actors must already be in a state of relaxed readiness. You need to have access to the outdoors, to areas that have differing terrains.

Find a location outdoors that is distinctive, and will allow a group to comfortably assemble (e.g. a large meadow, a small valley full of trees, the slope of a rocky hillside). You must now choose your "place" in this environment, and that means taking whatever place is appropriate both to the physical environment and in relationship to the other members of the group. This is not an intellectual exercise—such "choice" is indicative of what we intuitively do everyday as social animals, and is heightened and made profound by the care we now give to it.

Once everyone has found his/her place, a chosen leader can initiate an action—probably something as simple as walking to a new position. Because of the conscious inter-relatedness of the group, other members may now also need to shift position, and to find new placement within the environment, in relationship to the group. Honest action within this exercise can feel like a monumental shift, and only undertaken with courage and care.

Repeat this exercise three times in the same session, moving each time to a totally different environmental "space." You will find that some relationships change depending on the environment, and that Julie, who stands behind a tree near Frank in the valley, will isolate herself completely in the meadow. This exercise is done in silence. It is best to put aside several hours for its execution.

THE BLUEPRINT

A former student of mine, very concerned about making an important career decision, was calmed by her singing teacher's advice: "Don't you know that everything we do is already mapped out? Just follow the blueprint, darling." Every choice that we make is influenced by previous experience, and molded by our personality. For the actor, it is possible to see the correct "path," but not yet feel ready to take it. Honest perception of your path without the courage yet to follow is still the beginning of eventual achievement, and is its own kind of success. The blueprint is in your bones and awareness is the precursor to action.

Parallel walking exercise

Stand side by side with your partner and travel across the room. Your goal is to move in unison using exactly the same movements and at the same rate of motion. But you do not have the option to look at your partner in order to see what they are doing; instead, keep your focus directly in front of you.

After simply walking across the room (which can be done within these limitations with partial success), try varying the means of travel. No one said that you were limited to walking. Following natural trajectories of locomotion the body easily falls into bending, lunges, crawling, and myriad other varieties. Remember that either person can initiate the action—it is the responsibility of both partners to "listen" to the subtle physical shifts of the other. If you keep your focus soft, and honestly directed without cheating glances to the side, you will inevitably find yourself out of synchronicity at some point (for instance, you will initiate a step forward on the right foot, and suddenly become aware that they are lunging backward). Correct yourself without panic, forgive yourself immediately, and continue your unison journey. No one said you were going to be perfect. You will quickly find that moving slowly makes it easier to perceive and execute shared improvised movement. You will also find that working on different levels as you cross the floor makes it easier for you to use your peripheral vision.

Try this same exercise with three people, and notice how having a three-way partnership changes the dynamic of cueing as the middle person takes on a new importance as the conduit of action initiated from either side. Parallel walking can be visually engaging for the viewer, particularly when there are several couples crossing the room at once.

This exercise is useful on many levels. It demands a continuous focus relying partially on peripheral vision for physical cues. But it also demands a continuous "listening." In the physical equivalent to a good conversation, the strong physical actor must be engaged in achieving his/her goal (crossing the room), while focusing equal attention on their partner, intimately attentive to the slightest shift of weight or extension of their body. The most successful partners complement each other's activity, following through the natural trajectory of weight and energy established by the other (as opposed to trying to determine who is leading or taking conscious turns initiating movement).

In a good partnership it eventually becomes unclear who initiated a movement and who completed it. You willingly follow-through, always working with them, listening well, and perhaps even completing their sentence. Your job is to say "yes." Through practice and experience, a complicity of action emerges, and unexpected variations of motion rise up in the exchange.

Samurai warrior

This exercise develops co-ordination, quick physical reactions and the ability to maintain a strong physical position while moving through space. It is also a valuable aerobic exercise that wakes up the mind as well as the body.

You begin by designating a leader (the Lead Samurai Warrior) who faces the group holding an imaginary sword. This Japanese fighting weapon is held vertically in front of the body (like a jo or quarter staff). The group facing the leader all stand in second position plié, and wait absolutely still until they are cued by the Lead Warrior's movements to respond. The Lead Warrior swings the sword straight down in front of them and the entire group jumps backward (to avoid the blow), and then immediately jumps forward to their original places (still in second position plié). If someone fails to jump when the sword falls, they are "dead." The Lead Warrior turns to the left (facing profile) and brings the sword down again. The group jumps to the right. Besides slashing left or right, the Lead Warrior has two other death-dealing blows—to swing parallel to the ground at shoulder level (in which case the group ducks), and to kneel on one knee and swing (in which case the group jumps up). The Lead Warrior carefully demonstrates the five different sword techniques, and the group has a trial session of response, sometimes requesting corrections in the Lead Warrior's clarity of gesture. This is quickly accomplished, and now the real exercise can begin.

The goal of the Lead Warrior is to "kill" everyone as quickly as possible by a prescribed slash of the sword. The goal of the other

Samurai is to stay alive by reacting correctly and immediately to each sword stroke, jumping back to place before the next assault. If you fail in your response, you have the right to die dramatically, and then move to the side of the room to watch. The last person to be "killed" becomes the new Lead Samurai Warrior—all are resurrected, and a new assault begins.

Standard tactics for the Lead Warrior are speed, repetition with an unexpected variation, and alternating moves with no discernable pattern. However, all sword techniques must be executed with complete accuracy and clarity—the samurai were known for their integrity after all. As a participant in the group, you must be alert and in a state of relaxed readiness, ready to respond in an instant to attack from different directions. Of equal importance for the actor, you must keep a strong physical "center," able to move the entire body in space in a stable second position plié without any bending or breaking of position, and to do so with speed and accuracy.

Freeze frames

These exercises reveal the power of absolute stillness, and is a precursor of mimetic exercises oriented toward tension and release. Freeze frames are a collage of candid "photographs" showing improvised responses to a given circumstance within the boundaries of an externally dictated count. This work promotes physical responsiveness, co-ordinated follow-through of action, and the ability to work improvisationally within a rhythmic structure. This exercise is meant to be guided with a verbal count, and with strong visual images that suggest action.

A slow count of three (about one count a second) is verbally established by the leader "*and freeze*, two, three" with an emphasis on the "and freeze." Actors move only on the "and" and remain frozen in their final position for the duration of the count. Usually you begin with "three for nothing," a count of three where there is no movement and the beat is established.

Freeze frame exercise 1: physical extremes

Begin by taking your place in the space—once the count begins you take the most extreme position you can find on the first "and" (for example, standing on demi-point, arms and focus extended to the sky).

On the next "and" move to an opposite extreme (for example, lying flat on the floor). The movement must happen within the "and," and you will be "frozen" in your chosen extreme position for the duration of the count. You will find that your new position is dictated by the weight and equilibrium shift from the previous position. You will also find that a balance between absolute relaxation and absolute control is necessary in order to move at top speed and suddenly freeze in a new position. Along with that, you will see that the "and," contrary to initial perception, is enormous. There is plenty of time within the space between counts for an attentive, relaxed body to move to a spontaneous new extreme.

Run the exercise twelve to twenty times, and then show one or two examples. Actors must resist the temptation to re-create their most spectacular moves when "showing" work—they must instead remain in the moment, following immediate impulse, even with the added consciousness of performing for the group.

ABOUT SHOWING WORK

It is generally useful to share one or two improvisations with the rest of the group. These demonstration models sometimes epitomize the correct way an exercise should be done; usually they demonstrate one correct aspect of an exercise (the practitioners may be accurate in their freezes, or they may have wonderfully extreme positions). Whatever the reason work is shown, it must be discussed. Honing perceptions and sharing group observations is imperative. It is very important for the actor to learn from the outside by discovering what "worked" and what did not. We learn both by doing and by perceptively watching others. A major benefit of sharing physical work is that it trains the observers to "see."

Freeze frame exercise 2: given circumstances

This time you are working with guided imagery.

Imagine that you are walking down the street and see your best friend from childhood walking toward you. You have not seen each other in years. Take three for nothing and begin.

After twelve to twenty repetitions, show a successful practitioner to the group and talk about the discoveries made now that imagery is attached to the movements. You will quickly find that the eye of the viewer is quite discerning—an insincere "broadcasting" of emotion by the actor might be entertaining, but feels ultimately hollow and generic, and is far less engaging than in-the-moment physical response to the given circumstances.

One of the most difficult points early in practice is to hit the freeze "on the money," and it is worth achieving because a few things are achieved by this accuracy. The absolute stillness allows the frozen moment to resonate in the eye of the viewer. There is a visceral impact when a movement precisely stops and is absolutely frozen in space. We trust the information when it is unclouded and precise, and in the case of this exercise, we create an anticipation of the next action in the predictability of the count. As situational voyeurs, we have the opportunity to witness a brief emotional moment frozen long enough for us to study it in all its human complexity before it develops into the next display. As is true in most improvisation, the abandon of predictable outcome into which the courageous actor plunges themself is, ironically, the key to being able to control the movement. Abandon and control in this case implies both emotional availability and the attentive physical relaxation of an animal—a cat ready to pounce is potentially capable of extreme motion at any given moment, but only because the cat is in a state of relaxed alertness capable of responding to its given circumstances at the drop of a hat.

Freeze frame exercise 3: partnering with imagery

Stand side by side with a partner.

You are on a desert island with your partner, abandoned without food or water. Suddenly you see the rescue ship in the distance coming toward you. Three for nothing—one, two, three, *and freeze*.

Now that you are working with a partner, new challenges arise—and the extra stimulus of a partner's movements connected to intention creates an immediate need for physical and contextual response. Except that this is not always easy within the "and"—after repeating the exercise twelve to twenty times, watch a few partnering pairs and share observations.

It is important to remember that, although at an accelerated pace, these freeze frames are intended to be a sequence of candid photos—slices of life that show the awkward moments as well as the posed smiles. When someone calls me, I hear the voice, recognize my name, and then turn my head to respond. Although in very quick succession, these responses do not happen simultaneously. So also with freeze frames—your partner on the desert island may be grabbing your hand and lunging forward toward rescue, but you only register the intention and look out to sea in the "and." It will be the next freeze frame where you respond by jumping up and hugging your partner.

Pick up the exercise again.

You are still on the desert island, but despite your initial expectation, the rescue ship has not seen you. It is sailing away without you. Three for nothing—one, two, three, *and freeze*.

This reversal of fortune keeps the stakes high, and keeps you connected to your partner, your now inevitable companion into the foreseeable future stranded on this crummy island. It is important to remember to stay on the money with the counts, to hold the freezes immobile despite the high emotional content of the tableaux, and to listen to each other. Interestingly, if you are listening attentively to your partner and responding in the moment, even emotionally charged imagery such as the "desert island rescue," produces nicely balanced physical pictures full of instinctive counterbalance of levels, shapes and lines of direction.

Freeze frame exercise 4: intimacy

So far you have worked with extreme physicality and high emotion. Now try the same partnering exercise with a smaller but equally precise range of motion.

Begin sitting side by side with your partner on the floor.

You are at a junior high school assembly. It is 8am. The principal is talking. He is very boring. Three for nothing—one, two, three, *and freeze*.

You will find that movement is limited by the given situation—one is not supposed to do anything except sit quietly at a school assembly. Yet given the specifics of the circumstances (budding adolescence, boring principal, unsupervised activity), some expression or relationship to your partner or invisible classmates is inevitable.

After a few repetitions you will observe the power of a simple turn of your head toward your partner, or a quick dart of the eyes to see if your indiscretion is observed. The "and" is enormous, both in allowing for extreme movement and in creating a charged space for small expressive responses. Every movement counts, and the viewer is drawn into the clarity and simplicity of this exercise. As in previous versions, being accurately on the count, allows the viewer to relax and viscerally connect within the emotional/physical world you have created.

Other possible given circumstances for partnering freeze frames:

- You are on a blind date
- You are both on an obstacle course
- You are at a single's bar
- You are Berlin spies during the Cold War.

ABOUT PARTNERING

Generally partners choose each other, and then someone outside the group dictates the given circumstances. It always makes for interesting surprises. Partners change with each new repetition of an exercise. In a small group of eight to twelve, most actors will have the opportunity to work with at least half of their colleagues in a given session.

Freeze frames reveal the power of an honest emotional moment frozen in time. You improvise in expressive physicality, balanced between abandon and control. The alert practitioner learns how to maintain the correct amount of muscular tension in order to move quickly on impulse, and then abruptly freeze. The pleasure of pure creativity makes the freeze frames enjoyable to perform, and a sort of "instant art" for the viewer. A beneficial exercise dealing with the body in space and time, freeze frames are also a sort of bridge, introducing us to the creativity and stylistic control that is integral to mime.

CHAPTER 3

Mime

Why study mime?

Popularized in the 1960s by "mechanical robots" and subsequently demonized by a public oversaturated with white-faced mimics in city parks, mime has almost disappeared from contemporary consciousness. And perhaps it is a good thing that this art form has lost its generic charm.

As a tool for the working actor connecting intention to physical expressiveness, we return to mime in its essential form. The strong physical actor profits from the structure and vocabulary of mime isolations, a systematic breakdown of the body into separate working components. The mimetic elements of tension and release, counterbalance, immobility and action, and causality apply directly to movement for the stage. Combining these modalities with the vocabulary of isolations, the actor finds structural elements for a character, and creates physical characteristics. In addition, movement is connected specifically with intention and the specificity of gesture and thought gives the actor a clarity of action that is physically commanding. A former student of mine, when asked what had been the single most beneficial element of his movement training over a three-year period, replied without hesitation, "mime." The detailed articulations gave him vocabulary to play with and use in discovering physical characterization. You are also invited to play with the following isolations and articulations. Find what resonates in your body, and twist it, toy with it, and allow it to transform into useful characteristics. The physical actor who works with integrity can utilize isolations to externalize the heart of a character.

Mimetic modalities are also a precursor to our work in contact improvisation. Many of the exercises here can be seen as an end in themselves (with careful drilling of the wrist/hand articulations and modalities of tension and release and causality, you too can entertain your friends with mime illusions at parties). But we use the drill of illusions and study of mime modalities to indoctrinate our wise bodies. Like Pavlov's dog, we retain the experience of accuracy and specificity in our movement.

The following exercises are my personal synthesis of useful techniques for the actor taken from several different schools of mime. In the first part of this chapter I break down the body into basic isolations, with related exercises and guided improvisation. In the second part of the chapter we explore mime illusions, processing the modalities of causality and tension/release. We end with an exercise for slow motion, the elegance of the articulated body working in a state of perfect counterbalance.

Having discussed the theatrical benefits to be gleaned from technique and application, I must now mention that this chapter in no way presumes to layout fundamentals of any specific school of mime. Having studied with master mime/physical theater artists Etienne Decroux and Ella Jarosivitcz (Tomashevski technique) and having witnessed the studio work of Jacques Le Coq, Jean Dorcy, and Marcel Marceau during my training in Paris, I respectfully decline to summarize their years of physical research and separate techniques. The detailed exercises included here are my own synthesis of work that I have consistently found productive in the movement studio.

Alignment

Before isolating and controlling separate parts of the body, one must find a correctly aligned, neutral beginning point known as "perfect zero."

Start with a fully warmed-up body; stand facing the mirror and allow the body to collapse into "perfect ugliness." The pelvis tilts forward as the knees slightly bend, the chest naturally sinks back with the shoulders rounding forwards, and the chin and neck jutting straight out.

The entire body is thrown into a perfectly counterbalanced s-curve, pelvis and head equally distended, resembling a Cro-Magnum Human. You are perfectly balanced, and perfectly ugly. Turn sideways in the mirror and admire your perfect ugliness, making sure to retain the posture.

Walk in perfect ugliness. You will find that your steps remain small, feet barely picking up off the ground as the body maintains its supremely comfortable but dysfunctional position. Nod your head in greeting to the other perfectly ugly humans you see.

Return to your place in the room and turn profile to the mirror. Evolution is about to take place. Begin a slow undulation of the entire body, straightening the knees, which shifts the weight of the pelvis over the feet. As the spine undulates up the chest lifts, opening the shoulders, extending the line of energy up through the neck, lifting the head and allowing for free, easy motion through the entire body. Congratulations. You have reached confident, effortless humanity.

Walk through the room and notice that your weight remains centered and extended up through the spine allowing easy ambulation as the legs extend from hips that are no longer compacted. The pelvis is naturally aligned over the feet, and a small lift around the solar plexus extends the upper back and allows the shoulders to release without tension to the sides. The neck remains an extension of the spine, ending half-way up the cranium, allowing the head to balance effortlessly at the top.

Return to your place in front of the mirror and re-collapse into perfect ugliness again. Re-build vertebrae by vertebrae up from the knees, up through the spine and up off the top of the head, this time noting the undulation of energy that flows in a vertical line through the spine toward the sky. In this "perfect zero" you are now ready to isolate body parts.

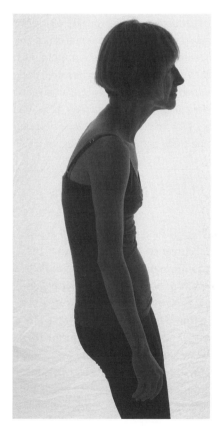
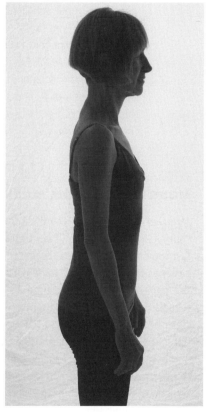

Isolations: to drill

There is no way around the fact that the following pages of technique are meant to be drilled. In as much as any physical discipline can be presented in a book, isolation vocabulary is presented here with hints and encouragement for successful execution. Direct application for the physical actor follows the technique section in exercises and improvisation based on this vocabulary.

About isolations: These are the fundamental building blocks of all mime techniques. In my experience Monsieur Decroux's system of isolations most specifically details body part with quality of motion ("engraving" or "soft" for instance) as well as orientation of the isolation (inclination, rotation, translation) and direction (right, left, forward, backward). For simplicity's sake, here I am presenting basic Tomaschevski isolations (as learned from Ella Jarosivitcz), articulating head, chest, pelvis, and shoulders in differing orientations. Isolations are best drilled in the mirror until the muscles "learn" how to accurately and consistently move the body part without the aid of visual correction.

MORE WORDS FROM JERRY

Jerry Letvin explained recent discoveries in his field concerning the act of signing one's signature. Twentieth-century science had assumed that the fast-moving neurons of the brain organized information and impulses in such a way as to dictate to the hand each tiny shift of pressure to form letters on the paper each and every time a name was signed. More recent research reveals that the hand itself memorizes the complex of movements needed to sign the name. After the initial "learning" process, the brain informs the hand of the task at hand, and the intelligent hand completes the task. Our bodies learn, and repeat learned behavior. In my experience, the early lessons of physical isolations remain engraved in our bodies, so extra care needs to be taken to program in the correct information at the start. I highly recommend initially working isolations using a mirror.

Isolations of the head

Inclinations

Release the head down, and back up.

Release to the right side, and up.

Release to back, and up.

Release to the left side, and up.

Circle the head slowly releasing front, side, back, and side.

Repeat.

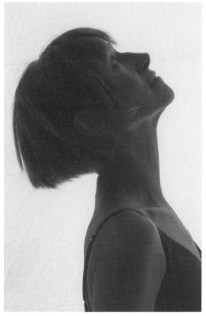

When allowing the head to "release" to the side, check back in the mirror, and make sure that "side" is truly to the side, and not tilted forward or backward. You should be able to see your face fully in the mirror when the head is inclined to the side. When releasing the head back, make sure to lift the chest slightly, allowing the neck to release without uncomfortably compacting the vertebrae. Each inclination of the head should be extended to its fullest range of motion. Accuracy is particularly important when first drilling isolations. So take the time to correct the movement now.

Repeat the isolations, this time starting in the opposite direction.

Repeat the two released circles at the end.

Make sure to hold the body immobile, using the minimum amount of tension necessary to extend up through the spine, isolating the head and neck in their activity. When isolating one part of the body, it is easiest to find a natural counterbalance "holding" tension in the opposite part of the body. For instance, imagine pulling down your left shoulder as you release your head to the right.

Translations forward and backward

Isolate forward (extending the neck, the face remaining fully frontal in the mirror).

Release back to center.

Isolate backwards (pulling the chin back into the neck, face remaining fully frontal).

Release back to center.

Imagine a large turtle extending its neck and pulling back into its shell.

Translate the head forward again, and hold this position of the head. Walk up to the mirror and study this "character." Now release the head center, translate to the back, and hold this position for observation. Rotate the head while translated forward or back,

 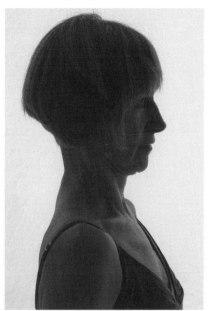

studying your reflection and mentally file this information away for future use.

The physical extremes found in isolations can be useful building blocks for strong physical character choices, and stylized commedia del'arte and mask personages.

Translations to the side

Isolate the head to the right side (imagine the left shoulder anchored in place as you push the right ear over the right shoulder, face fully frontal in the mirror).

Release to center.

Isolate the head to the left side (imagine the right shoulder anchored in place as you push the left ear over the left shoulder).

Release to center.

Side translations of the head are difficult, so apologies to all 1950s Hollywood Siamese depictions.

Place praying hands over your head and try to isolate the head to the side again. Move without stopping from a left to right side translation. Concentrate on holding the shoulders in direct opposition, watching your progress in the mirror.

Now release the hands and go back to the original exercise with a better understanding of the muscles needed to initiate motion and the opposite tension needed to maintain the isolation.

Rotations

Turn the head to the right side.

Return to center.

Turn the head to the left side.

Return to center.

Repeat these rotations, keeping the head on a steady plane as it turns to the side. You can cheat here by looking in the mirror as you rotate the head, making sure that it turns exactly to the side without inclining up or down in the process.

Now we will change the rhythm of this movement, turning the head slowly, consistently, in a fully extended rotation. And stop.

The "stop" is very important for isolations, and most easily demonstrated in this rotation. A little extra impulse of tension abruptly

"stops" the motion, a sudden breaking of your trajectory. This stop is useful as a clear delineation of action, and gives the movement importance in the eye of the viewer. Action is deliberately begun and ended.

LESSONS FROM ETIENNE DECROUX

As a young training actor, my work with Monsieur Decroux left me with a complex system of physical vocabulary that I cannot claim to have mastered, and some fundamental concepts of movement that have resonated in all my subsequent work. Probably the most significant is acknowledging the importance of every movement. Nothing is gratuitous. Each conscious movement resonates, "incised in space" and is chosen and executed with this knowledge. A colleague of mine, the popular American pantomime Trent Arterberry, when asked what had been the hardest thing for him to master in his training, replied "standing still."

Rotation with eyes

Turn the gaze of your eyes to the right side.

Turn your head to join the same direction as your eyes.

Turn the gaze of your eyes to the center (leaving your head rotated right).

Turn your head back to the center to join the direction of your eyes.

Repeat to the left.

Normally in head isolations, the eyes travel with the body. In this case we add an extra complexity to the simple head rotation. A whole new emotional connotation is implied with this double isolation. Although the head is clearly occupied elsewhere, the active eyes move separately, pulling the head to a new location, literally re-focusing its attention. Technically it is important to once again keep the eyes and head on the same plane, accurately moving to the side and center, and stopping cleanly.

Double take

We now take the simple head rotations and add rhythm and intention.
Turn your head slowly to the right, stop.

Slowly turn back to center, stop (imagine that you are casually looking at something, and barely registering the observation, you turn back complacently).

"What did I see?"—quickly shake your head back and forth in tiny top-speed rotations (suddenly you realize that you've just seen your house burning down).

Quickly turn your head back to the right, stop (confirm that your house is on fire).

Turn your head back to center.

Repeat the same sequence to the left, resisting the temptation to make physical faces, "showing" your emotion.

Allow the movement to express the complacency, then urgency and shock of the situation. Keep the specificity of the action, maintaining motion on a consistent plane, and stopping accurately, even in the double take.

Stand side by side with a partner, and execute the same sequence of movements, but this time rotating your head in your partner's direction.

The movement now takes on a whole new meaning, as your partner is now your focus, and the cause of your double take. The simplicity of the motion, executed cleanly by two people with identical timing is engaging for the viewer. Once again, the accuracy of motion and rhythm (as noted in the freeze frame exercises, pp. 48–53) allows the spectator to kinetically absorb the relationship.

Repeat the same sequence, this time turning away from your partner, and note the new implied connotations.

Change partners, and run the sequence in both directions.

Note how the impact changes for the viewer depending on the height, gender, and size difference between you and your partner. The movement sequence has not changed, the intention has not changed, but the set-up has intrinsic implications, and the set-up has changed.

Isolations of the shoulder

Translations

Shoulders are expressively articulated in Tomaschevski technique. The shoulders rotate forward and backward, up and down, in and out, and unlike isolations of the chest, pelvis, and head, they can also isolate separately.

Pick both shoulders up (imagine strings attached to the shoulders pulling them straight up).

Release back to center (imagine the strings cut).

Pull down—this isolation engages lateral muscles of the upper back (imagine a weight pushing the shoulders down).

Release back to center (take off the weight).

Repeat four times.

Alternate shoulders in the same exercise, doubling your speed.

Pick the right shoulder up.

Pick the left shoulder up.

Release the right shoulder back to center.

Release the left shoulder back to center.

Pull the right shoulder down.

Pull the left shoulder down.

Release the right shoulder back to center.

Release the left shoulder back to center.

Repeat twice, and then repeat the original double shoulder exercise.

If there is any ambiguity about where to articulate, try the same isolation with the arms extended straight up above the head, remembering to keep the chest separated from the shoulders.

Rotation

Pick both shoulders up and rotate forward.

Pick both shoulders up and return back to center.

Pick both shoulders up and rotate back.

Pick both shoulders up and return back to center.

Notice that we "pick the shoulders up" initiating the isolation by first separating the area, then moving it.

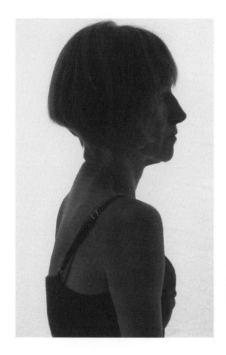
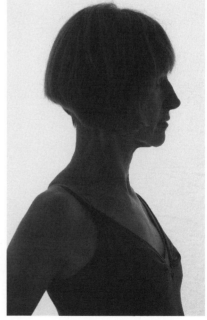

Now, as in the last exercise, repeat separating the shoulders.

Pick up the right shoulder and rotate forward.

Pick up the left shoulder and rotate forward.

Pick up the right shoulder and return back to center.

Pick up the left shoulder and return back to center.

Pick up the right shoulder and rotate back.

Pick up the left shoulder and rotate back.

Pick up the right shoulder and return back to center.

Pick up the left shoulder and return back to center.

Repeat twice, and then repeat again using both shoulders.

Find the rhythm in the sequence, picking up the pace and using only the musculature necessary to isolate the shoulders, leaving the chest immobile.

Isolations of the chest

Translations forward and backward: from perfect zero

Imagine the top of the ribcage and push this forward (p. 70).

Return to center.

Imagine pushing the area between the shoulders straight back (p 70).

Return to center.

It is important to keep the torso stable and lifted around the solar plexus, and to keep the shoulders immobile in order to execute this difficult isolation. Useful imagery is a string attached to the breastbone pulled forward and another attached to the area between the shoulder blades pulling back.

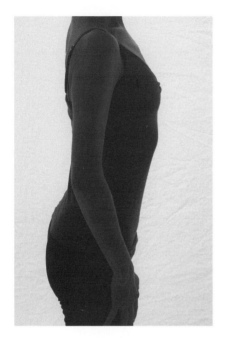 

Translations to the side

Push the chest to the right side (p. 71).

Return to center.

Push the chest to the left side (p. 71).

Return to center.

Keep the torso lifted and anchor the pelvis in place as a counter-balance to this chest isolation. The chest can be a difficult area to impulse in isolation in any direction. Do not hesitate to put hands on hips as a reference, or to manually push the ribcage to the side when first discovering which muscles are needed to isolate this movement. Avoid letting the chest "cave in" or the spine release.

Now try combining chest isolations:

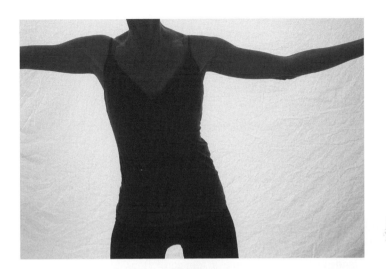

Translate forward.

Return to center.

Translate to the right side.

Return to center.

Translate to the back.

Return to center.

Translate to the left side.

Return to center.

Circle the chest clockwise, forward, side, back, and side.

Circle counterclockwise and return to center.

Repeat the entire sequence starting to the left.

Pelvis: inclinations

Stand in a second position plié, feet comfortably turned out, and legs a minimum of shoulder width apart. Remember that plié in French means "to bend," and you should remain in second position plié as you execute this isolation.

Tilt the pelvis forward and up, and return to center.

Tilt the pelvis to the right side, and return to center.

Tilt the pelvis back (like a duck), and return to center.

Tilt the pelvis to the left side, and return to center.

Circle the pelvis clockwise, and repeat counterclockwise.

Repeat the entire sequence.

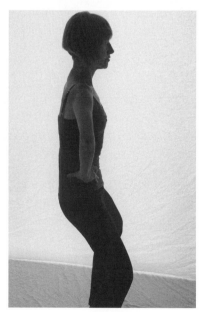

Again remind yourself that the rest of the body remains immobile, effortlessly lengthened and simultaneously relaxed as you find the isolation and push it to its maximum extension without engaging any unnecessary musculature.

Direct application: improvisation

Bus stop improvisation

Use any and all of the simple head isolations we have already explored and stand side by side with your partner. These head isolations are the only means of communication that you have available to you in the following situation:

You are waiting for a bus. It is very late at night and there is no one else on the street, except this person standing next to you. It is a very bad part of town.

Three for nothing, one, two, three.

This situation is charged; suddenly simple head isolations take on a whole new impact with implied emotional connotations. Avoidance, curiosity, attraction, repulsion, fear, and potential complicity are witnessed as partners relate within this context using only head isolations of varying speed and rhythm. Once again, accuracy in execution clarifies intention, and good listening is imperative. The bus stop exercise is surprisingly rich—complex relationships are developed by the honest practitioners and we see the importance of every movement. Less is more.

Isolation circle toss exercise

One of the most active dynamic concepts for the physical actor is the use of action/reaction. I often use this exercise in preparation for any work in mime partnering improvisation.

Stand in a circle. One of the players makes eye contact and "tosses" a head isolation to you. You "catch" it, and pass it on to another player in the circle, initiating your toss with a head isolation of your choice.

Action demands reaction, and a fast forward translation of the head needs to be caught by a fast backward translation of the head. Match their rhythm, and counterbalance their action, much as you would in an exaggerated game of catch. Toss head isolations around the circle, making eye contact before the action.

Now the impulse is in your chest—play with these variations, once again passing the chest isolation in its many forms around the circle. Causality is key: you are not mirroring your partner, you are responding to them.

After exploring head, chest, and pelvis (and inevitably pelvis isolations are both the most silly and the most accurate), you are going to combine them in a single round. Jack throws Jill a chest translation forward, and she catches it in a chest translation backward. The ball is now literally in her court, and after catching, she allows the impulse to transform in her body. It re-emerges as a head isolation to the side, which she tosses to another player in the circle. The creative actor will find many possibilities using the isolations already explored—and then find further expressiveness in knees, elbows, and shoulders. The action/reaction partnership is paramount, and well-played responsiveness has an almost visceral impact. You feel the energy passed between the two bodies, both as executor and as observer.

The only boundaries to this improvisation are that you need to catch with the same isolation as was used in the throw, and that you need to receive with the same velocity and intensity. Enjoy digesting a catch, and allow it to transform into an impulse in a new part of the body. Good physical listening, a certain expertise with isolations, and a sense of causality in action are skills developed with this exercise. An additional bonus is a sense of playfulness and freedom to be found within the perimeters of technique.

Conversation between body parts improvisation 1

In this exercise you are in conversation with a partner—the only restrictions are that this dialogue take place between two separate parts of the body. Your shoulder is in conversation with their foot. Go.

The set-up for enjoyable ridiculousness is obvious—but, in fact, communication between attentive and creative actors working within these boundaries can be sophisticated. The shoulder may be shy, the foot may be aggressive, and each nuance of exchange between partners grounded in these parts of the body surprisingly parallels verbal conversation. Subtlety and nuance of motion and rhythm play a major role in communication. Similar to the circle toss exercise, you are limited in locality of expression, but this time you explore physicalized emotional reaction to your partner's action. Exact isolation opposition is not necessary (and sometimes it is not even anatomically possible). The improbable extremes of body parts are fun to explore (indeed, vocabulary common to foot and shoulder is not immediately obvious). Feel free to use other parts of your body (your head watches, your legs move you closer), but real communication is still expressed primarily between shoulder and foot.

Conversation between body parts improvisation 2

Another way the creative actor can utilize this exercise is to go from this play between autonomous extremes to a play between personages who have identifiable characteristics centered in these body parts. For instance a 1920s flapper in a bar might use her shoulder expressively to get the attention of the sullen guy tapping his foot and drinking a beer. These characters can move more than their foot and shoulder—the flapper may also be smoking a cigarette, the guy might be pulling change from his pocket—but the real communication between these two people takes place between foot and shoulder.

(The flapper slowly turns to look at the drinker, her shoulder subtlety rises, and after a pause she looks away and leans her chin on her hand. The shoulder slowly rotates in, closing her off for the moment. The drinker feeling her gaze has turned to look at her. His foot slowly stops tapping as they lock eyes. When she turns away, he hitches up his trousers, crosses his legs, foot dangling, and takes another sip of beer.)

Try the exercise again, this time allow the isolation to dictate a character. Now work with characters that communicate via these body parts.

Body parts should be dictated randomly to working partners, and usually the body part will "create" the character, and the combination of characters will create the relationship. Chest, pelvis, shoulder, and head are obvious choices for isolatable body parts, but as in the circle toss exercise, do not feel confined to defined vocabulary—the action/reaction between partners is the critical dimension of communication.

ISOLATIONS CONNECTED TO EMOTION AND SENSE PERCEPTION

Many schools of mime give emotional connotations to specific areas of isolations. A general rule of thumb for Tomaschevski-based work is as follows:

Motion initiating from the head implies an action connected to the senses or intellect. For instance my head translates to the side when I "hear" someone call my name. I "see," "smell," "taste," and "think" with the head. Combinations of pure designs of the head are then possible; you rotate your head to the side noticing a flower, and then translate it forward to smell its elusive perfume. Isolations of the chest imply emotion—literally action emanating from the heart. We run through a field of flowers, chest forward and arms open to meet our true love who is waiting in the middle. We walk sadly, chest sunken when depressed, or we recoil, chest leading the rest of the body back, when repulsed by the leering pirate. Isolations of the pelvis imply sexuality, sensuality, or "earthiness." The cowboy walks bow-legged pelvis tilted forward, the hooker leads with hips. A pelvis tilted down or pushed back inhibits freedom of locomotion and implies a restricted or repressed sexuality.

Isolation leading exercise

Experiment with these very general rules of thumb connecting emotion to isolations.

Cross the room, initiating your locomotion with three different head isolations. For instance, you spot a friend in a crowd, and head leading forward in eagerness, you walk toward them. After a few steps release the image and the physicality and go back to perfect zero. A new impulse takes over as you "hear" an elusive bird. Follow the sound, a side translation of the head leading the action, and then release back again to perfect zero. Explore a final isolation, as the absented-minded professor lost in an idea, walks with his head tilted to the side toward his classroom. These are suggestions —your wise body will find others as you connect perception to head isolations.

Try the same exercise, this time using your emotions (centered in your chest) to initiate the motion.

Cross the room with three different variations of sensuality/sexuality initiated by your pelvis.

These should all be explored with gusto and playfulness to their extremes and also in potential subtleness. Not every attempt will work, but so what? The only way to find useful vocabulary is to take the specific techniques and, by exploring, make them your own.

Mannequin exercise

This is a classic mime exercise from which any number of mime scenarios have evolved involving mechanical beings, robots, and immobility vs. mobility. We use it here to further understand the power of stillness, and as a direct application of the articulations of the body learned in the practice of isolations.

Stand with your partner. They are next to you in perfect zero and will not move from this position until cued by you. Your job is to manipulate them joint by joint into any position you would like. Begin by working with obvious articulations of arms, head, wrists, and knees. The chest can rotate, incline, or translate with appropriate pressure on the ribcage. The torso can bend at the waist. The entire body can be pivoted by the clever manipulator who transfers full weight over one leg and then swivels the extended body to face another direction. Experiment with the amount of force used to achieve these articulations as well as where it is applied. Obvious articulations of the limbs at shoulder, elbow, hip, and knee are easier to manipulate than the pelvis or chest. You quickly see that gentle, steady pressure at a focal point of articulation yields easy results.

Meanwhile it is equally important that the mannequin maintain position, and this is done by keeping the sense of elongation observed in perfect zero, simultaneously extended *and* released. If a mannequin is holding a position in absolute muscular tension, there is no way to move them. The mannequin must be available to manipulation, and yet controlled enough to move only the part of the body cued to move. Of course, interesting experiments in extremes will inevitably take place, but the attentive manipulator will quickly learn how far a partner's balance and strength can be pushed. Be kind to your partner, and do not ask them to maintain impossible equilibrium, because retaliation is coming.

Switch roles.

Anyone who has played with dolls or action figures will remember the pleasure of manipulating an inanimate object into creative positions. Manipulation also means understanding "how" something works, and whether it is plastic, clay, or, in this case, muscle and bone, the only way you can easily control a physical form is to find its innate maneuverability. Within the human body, unlike plastic supermen, there is not equal resistance in each joint. Part of the pleasure of this exercise is further noting the varying resistance and compliance in different joints, and working within their natural range. Building on the mannequin exercise, we now explore expressive positions of the articulated body, and how they are interpreted by the observer.

Statuary garden exercise

You are working once again with a partner, and your goal is to create a statue, using them as your "clay." This statue will reflect an emotional state of heroic proportions, much like statues in formal gardens. Your topic is "Triumph," and remembering that sculpture is a three-dimensional art, this statue should read as "Triumph" even from the back. You have three minutes. Go.

When the three minutes is up, the statues remain frozen in position, and the sculptors tour the sculpture garden, studying the displayed statues from all angles. When the tour is complete, the sculptures release, and observations are exchanged.

You will quickly see commonalities in statues with the same emotional attributes. In Triumph, the posture is upright, the chest is lifted, and the general line of energy is open, expansive, and strong. Triumph implies overcoming adversity. These general physical manifestations are good to observe, discuss, and file away for future use. Though specifics may change somewhat from culture to culture or in different time periods, an audience generally sees certain postures as reflecting specific emotional states.

Looking more closely in detail, we remember that every movement counts, and a sculpture is a combination of hundreds of small distinct movements frozen in time. The fingers of the left hand are clenched in determination, the weight is shifted to the front of the foot extending the body slightly forward and up. The head is inclined to the right, and lifted, the eyes focused into the far distance. Change any one of these details and the whole picture is somewhat altered. The only way to find adjustments that signify is to experiment with the topic in mind. What is triumph to you? The embodiment of your beliefs, experience, and observations are sculpted onto your partner. You have felt triumph, how does it materialize? Interestingly, it is often easiest to see these small emotional/physical adjustments mapped onto someone else.

How do we epitomize triumph, even from the back? Obviously an articulation using more than facial expression is a good beginning. Articulations upward of the chest and head and opening of the shoulders are seen from the back as well as the front. But as sculptors have known since the Renaissance, dynamism is well expressed in counterbalance of the body. Circles and spirals of energy not only show a ready muscularity, but also imply emotion in their counterbalance of tension. Triumph soars, and the eye is caught, not just by the linear upward movement, but also by the implication of recent struggle resolved, and intention moving skyward.

A secondary benefit of the statuary exercise is the experience of the person being sculpted. An available spirit, in addition to a pliable body, is key to further discovery. As you are manipulated, chest lifted, one palm open, shoulders released, you begin to feel triumphant. Certainly the release of muscular tension, and natural extension of the spine contribute to this feeling of well-being, but there is a further contribution of muscle memory. The popular adage of the 1950s, "smile if you feel low, and you will soon be happy," originally referred to the benefits of maintaining a positive attitude, but we know now that there are physiological responses in the body that contribute to the truth of this saying. The physical self remembers emotions connected to posture. A triumphant sensation can be evoked with an uplifted chest and arm, just as the muscles of the face employed in a smile can trigger emotions of happiness. The emotionally available actor can feel the nuance of emotion when manipulated in certain positions, and eventually feel emotional connotations in subtle shifts. You will "feel" when the position is right.

Explore other statuary themes (*grief*, *ecstasy*, and *greed* are interesting subjects), noting external implications of positioning and internal sensations as form is mapped onto you.

We gain a lot from the statuary exercise—continued reliance on the sensitivity of our partners, experience in maintaining stillness and simultaneous relaxation, but more importantly we become familiar with conscious expressive positioning. We see from the outside how physical expression reads to the viewer, and we have the opportunity to experience from the inside, how it "feels." Isolations have become the reliable physical vocabulary of the expressive actor.

Mime illusions: articulated action

Hand and wrist articulations working in tension and release create many familiar pantomime "illusions" (for example, "the wall," "pulling a rope," Marceau's famous "butterfly"). The physical actor studying mime encounters the dynamics of tension and release, causality, and counterbalance. Illusionary mime is a combination of isolations/articulations and these dynamics. We all delight in illusionary pantomime technique, and the practitioner gets a little immediate gratification in the execution and mastery over an imaginary world. In exploring mime illusions, you gain expressiveness in fine motor control, as well as useful partnering dynamics. The articulated action of mime is, in fact, a precursor to the dynamic relationships in contact improvisation.

Hand and wrist articulation exercises

Shake the hands, throwing them off the wrist, fingers released. The fully released fingers will slap against each other. Now quickly rotate the wrists, again allowing relaxation in fingers and noting the biceps are also released and flabby. Take this full relaxation of hand and wrist and throw it out, finger pointed, into perfect full tension.

Repeat, playing with the positioning of this accusatory finger in space, always throwing it out with full relaxation into full tension.

Release again into the fast relaxed wrist rotation, and this time throw the entire hand out splaying fingers and focusing tension by pushing the knuckle of the hand down.

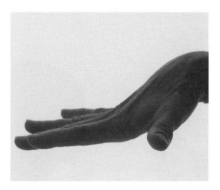

The hand will not be absolutely flat, in fact it will be slightly concave, but in the illusionary mime world this controlled extreme gives the impression of flatness.

Improvise with this articulation imagining a laser beam extending from the fingertips. Release the hand into a gentle shake, and suddenly throw the energy out the fingertips, in the direction of an unsuspecting victim.

Release again, and repeat the attack on a new victim.

While enjoying your newfound power, note that the only way to move quickly from absolute relaxation to absolute tension is to have a focal point of tension to stop the movement at its extreme. And that focal point is the knuckle.

Wall illusion

This action of throwing the hand to full controlled extension is an exercise in tension and release, but it is also the fundamental action used in all illusions defining walls, ceilings, and doors. Feel free to explore planes in space as defined by "flat" hand placement on the imaginary surfaces.

The hand splays down in full knuckle tension on the surface, and then releases away from the surface. Sequential hand placement

is critical (i.e. do not lift both hands off of the illusionary wall at the same time) and make sure to keep both hands on the same plane. This will initially take practice using the mirror. Technique combined with creative belief (you must respect the wall as if it is real) is the essence of illusionary mime.

Small object drop illusion

With the first finger and thumb of the right hand, dangle a small imaginary object (a key for instance) over the waiting palm of the left hand.

Drop it, opening first finger and thumb. The left hand "catches" the key in the middle of the palm—the knuckles this time pulling down with the illusionary weight of the object, and the fingers staying straight.

Retrieve the key with the right hand; the knuckles of the left palm slowly move back to their original position as the object is drawn back up to dangle enticingly above the palm.

Play with the timing of action/reaction throw and subsequent catch. The heavier the object, the faster and deeper the catch. Inversely, if the object is now a tiny feather, you elongate the amount of time it takes to travel to the waiting palm and reduce the moment of impact to a small but concise action.

Mime illusions are exaggerated realities: the observer "sees" the invisible object because of the exaggeration in physical properties. The convex extended palm appears straight, and the extreme causality in the drop and response seems playfully appropriate.

Ball drop illusion

Take the same basic action and the same sense of causality, but this time with a larger object. Because the object is larger and heavier, the implied weight is no longer shown by the knuckles, it is shown by the wrist.

The right hand holds an imaginary ball; it is important that the hand shows the shape of the ball and not merely the action of holding. (In Tomaschevski technique this is known as "body identification with object." Your hand IS the ball, and it is also, simultaneously, the hand throwing it.)

Release the ball, knuckles extended in the action, to show a now empty hand. In reaction, the wrist of the left hand drops, as the heavy ball is caught (fingers of course curved perfectly around this imaginary object).

Pick the ball back up and, as in the small object drop, the empty hand slowly straightens out as the object is raised back to original position.

Experiment with this new focus of weight and energy exchange, and play with the force with which you drop/throw the ball, and the corresponding reaction in the catch. Now, instead of retrieving the ball, throw it back up, and explore the action/reaction in both directions as the ball travels down, and then is thrown back up again.

You now have the basic technique to throw illusionary balls from any direction (if you rotate your hand position, you can also toss from one side to the other). Action of the throw demands a reaction in the catch, and you have the basic concept of energy exchange and causality articulated in this hand/wrist illusion. Now let's involve the rest of the body.

Ball throw to the sky illusion

Stand with knees slightly bent, holding your ball, and throw it straight up into the air. As you throw, the entire arm engages, releasing the ball from the hand and wrist. Simultaneously the spine undulates up straightening the knees—the line of energy upward initiates the release of the ball. The arm participates in this throw upward, a natural sequential extension of the undulation of pelvis, chest, and head. The head is inclined forward and up watching the trajectory of the ball, the whole body suspended in this position of upward release.

But not for long. As the ball falls, the flat hand waits to catch it, and the moment of impact is seen in the hand (knuckles pulling down wrist and arm), the chest (translated slightly back with the force of the catch), and finally in the knees (slightly bent again as the body absorbs the catch). This sequence of action, of course, all happens

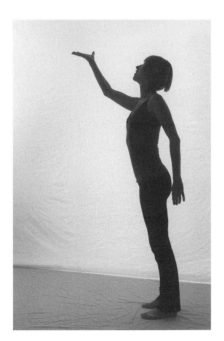
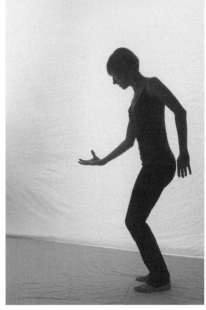

very quickly, and the physical logic of the causality is felt by performer and observer.

Ball toss side to side illusion

Explore this skyward toss and then experiment tossing the ball from side to side with this same sense of full body articulation combined with the hand/wrist articulation. As you forcefully throw, the impact of the catch is shown in quick succession by the wrist pulling the arm straight, extending the shoulder, and finally pulling the chest into a full side translation.

A really forceful throw will also engage the pelvis, pulling the full body weight, knee bent, over to one side. A released head and neck reverberate with the impact, as they, too, are dragged into response by the force of the throw.

Ball toss improvisation

Work with a partner. You have two people and one ball. Go.

The sky is the limit and you use your full set of tools to articulate response to your partner's action. The articulated body is now fully engaged as a part of the illusionary action/reaction ball toss. Remember, as in the isolation toss exercise, you need to respond to the exact direction and velocity of their throw. Causality between partners throwing this invisible energy back and forth is palpable. Attentive responsiveness is developed using technique and dynamics that are now slowly becoming your own.

SLOW MOTION

Peter Brook, unquestionably one of the most influential Western theater directors of the second half of the twentieth century, was in residency at the Bouffes du Nord Theater in Paris in the late 1970s. As a young student in Paris working with the great mime masters on acquisition of a primarily static vocabulary, I was drawn to the dynamism of Peter Brook's legendary productions. When word got out among the mime students that he was holding a public demonstration of company research, I was determined to witness this work and perhaps speak to the great man himself. I had been told that he was approachable (though no one I knew had actually spoken to him). In fact the only personal information that I had about him was that he often wore an orange sweater.

On the day of the presentation, I found my way with difficulty to the theater in an obscure section of Paris, and on opening the door found a few hundred well-dressed and cultured patrons already ahead of me. I took my seat, and looked around, hoping to catch a glimpse of the noted director. Suddenly, and without introduction, the theater company assembled onstage led by several Japanese monks who conducted them in a silent demonstration of exercises dealing primarily in partner work in weight and energy exchange. The company actors were totally committed, seemingly unaware of the audience, and I was mesmerized. (I later found out that these were mostly aikido exercises.) At the end of the demonstration (which ended as it began without lecture or explanation) the actors silently filed out of the theater, followed by the audience. Where was the great Peter Brook? I eagerly watched as several men of presence and confidence greeted other spectators and then joined the crowd filing slowly out; clearly he was in hiding. Finally, there were only two other people left in the theater—the musician packing up his instruments, and the janitor picking up programs. It was only as I walked toward the door that I realized that the janitor was wearing a worn grey sweater that had at one time been orange.

The three-minute sit was one of the lessons I learned that day.

The three-minute sit

Asian influence in Western movement theater training (often seen via butoh dance, the martial arts of tai chi and aikido, and Buddhist meditation techniques) brings the benefits of directed action, relaxed control, and the natural elegance of the human body working in counterbalance.

You stand in perfect zero. Your goal is to move from this position to a sitting position on the floor in one long, continuous action, without any change in your rate of motion. You will have three minutes to accomplish this task. As preparation, find the most comfortable way for your body to go from standing to sitting, and practice this a few times. When you are satisfied with your trajectory, stand in a relaxed perfect zero for a few moments. Someone will be timing you and letting you know when one minute is up, two minutes, and three minutes.

The clock is ticking. Go.

Very quickly practitioners of this exercise see that whatever trajectory they have chosen, it does not allow the muscles to continuously support the weight of the body. You speed up when the trembling quads fighting gravity can no longer support the steady downward weight of the torso, and you slow down again when moving extremities. The eyes tend to move ahead of the body, and balance is suddenly shaky as a movement that normally takes two seconds is now executed in three long minutes.

Try moving again from standing to sitting, but this time allow the body to find the easiest way to move, allowing gravity this time to work for you. You will find that to permit the body to function most economically, you will use the minimum amount of tension necessary to maintain balance and position. And you will also allow the body to turn. Spiral action downward is useful in establishing counterbalance, allowing weight to re-distribute as you descend. Allow the arms to support the weight of the body if opportunity arises. Accept the unexpected but natural inclinations to the side as gravity and weight seek support in the capable skeleton. As we will explore in contact improvisation, part of a good contactor's job is taking responsibility for their own weight—understanding the use of the skeleton as an integral structure that allows one to support weight without muscular strength. It is not all in the muscles; we move from an internal structure of bone that was created for maximum efficiency. We are, after all, human animals, and looking for the easiest possible locomotion.

Try the three-minute sit a third time. Now with greater relaxation and use of rotation in the descent, you will find yourself moving more consistently, and fluidly shifting weight with the minimum amount of effort. You also find yourself in "impossible" positions, as the body is perfectly counterbalanced, the entire elongated torso balanced on one hand, or an outstretched leg sliding into a spiral downward. The viewer takes pleasure in the consistent, ever-changing harmony of a moving counterbalanced body. The sense of focus in continuous action makes this exercise a physical meditation, reminding us to release into our weight following the natural lines of energy and structure innate within our bodies.

CHAPTER 4

Partnering

1. One who shares or is associated with another in some action or endeavor; sharer, associate. . . . 5. One's companion in a dance. 6. A player on the same team.

Webster's Dictionary

This chapter explores the ability to manipulate and control the flow of weight and momentum of another person. The physical actor embraces the "other" as a companion in the dance and a player on the same team. You will execute simple exercises focused on how to release your body onto the supportive floor and balanced up into the air. Your "sharer in the endeavor" will exchange roles with you as "base" and "flier," providing a secure foundation and, alternately, an elegantly maneuverable body.

The ability to shift effortlessly between responsive and active roles is the physical actor's goal, so by understanding and practicing these primary principles and techniques of weight manipulation even the most petite woman can lift the largest guy in the room. Partnering techniques lead us from the specifics of expressive isolations to activities that rely on spontaneous adaptation to the other. Work with different partners and respect their individual structure, weight, and energy.

Below are explanations of simple weight-sharing exercises (taken from aikido, dance, and other contact practitioners) and a useful arc of practice. Size, weight, and age extremes demand thoughtful partnering in some of the work, but it can generally be done by anyone who is comfortable executing the warm-up sequence. These exercises are essential preparation for the actor's contact improvisation.

The arc and the exercises

Exercises oriented toward similar goals are laid out in groups. You pick and choose which exercises to execute in a given session. The listings in each group are progressively more demanding, as is the order of groups. Exercises are most effective if executed in the order outlined (one good thing leads to another).

Group 1 exercises: weight and counterbalance

Exercise 1: standing

Sit on the floor facing your partner and take each other's wrists. Lean away, and using each other's weight as ballast, stand.

Depending on the weight and size of your partner, you will need to bend at the waist or knees or both, counterbalancing your weight with theirs.

Go back down to sitting, still pulling away from your partner. Repeat the sequence a few times.

Exercise 2: stretching backs

Begin in standing position. Continue to hold wrists, pull away from your partner bending the knees slightly, rounding the back, and tucking the pelvis under. Push your navel back. This should pleasantly stretch the lumbar region of the lower back. Feel free to gently shift the weight from one side of the lower back to the other, using your partner as a tree or a jungle gym to find the optimum stretch for you.

Lean away stretching the upper back and shoulders, pushing the area between your shoulders back. Gently explore small shoulder rotations, and little twists to the side.

You will soon discover an important guideline to weight exchange—every movement you make affects your partner. Your slight twist is counterbalanced by an equal redistribution of weight and position on their part. Allow your body to naturally move in opposition; it is the easiest possible way to maintain equilibrium, otherwise you are both knocked off balance. (Giving weight is an essential element of contact improvisation, and you can easily counterbalance a partner twice your size by positioning your body to support their weight.)

Explore these subtle positioning shifts. Note how heavy or light you become by straightening or bending knees, alternately tucking the pelvis under or leaning away with upper back and shoulder stretches.

Try the same exercise with one hand (right hand to right hand), exploring sideways twists and stretches.

Switch hands.

You will find obvious, mutual counterbalance, because as you explore, your partner explores too. You are in a symbiotic, mutually beneficial relationship.

Exercise 3: stretching backs variation, working with a base

One person works as the base, as the other person leans away in a one arm, one leg weight exploration.

Even as an immovable anchor, you will need to counterbalance and shift weight as your partner experiments with outstretched legs and arms and more or less ballast is needed. A low pelvis, dropped down and pulled back, makes you a stable base, and small people anchoring big people will find this position useful.

Switch arms, and then switch roles.

As you boldly explore full extensions of legs with bent or straight knees, pulling away from your base, you note that sudden shifts of weight knock you or your partner off balance. Be bold but be slow, allowing them to readjust in response as you move to a new extreme.

In any case, if you do fall over, the ground is only inches away.

Exercise 4: stretching backs variation, working with suspension

As in Exercise 2, begin by leaning away from your partner, right hand to right hand, bending the knees to tuck the pelvis under. There should be tension in your right arm. Take three small bounces in this position, and switch hands. Repeat this a few times, noting the moment of suspension in the change of hands.

Accentuate that moment of suspension by pulling your partner toward you, the bodies coming almost up to standing, switch hands, and release the weight back again. Play with synchronizing the moment of tension as you pull your bodies up. The bounce is there to facilitate the count.

Try pulling up and allow a moment of free-fall suspension before catching hands and falling back again.

The mutual tension in supporting arms gives control, and allows the body to use the weight and momentum of the movement to maximum benefit. One of the primary lessons of contact improvisation is understanding how to utilize a partner's momentum, velocity, and weight to mutual benefit.

Group 2 exercises: weight support (skeleton)

Exercise 1: front over back

You are about to support your partner's full weight, but this time you use your skeleton as the primary structure of support. For this exercise find a partner who is about your weight and height.

Stand directly in front of your partner, both facing the same direction, and take hold of their wrists, stretching their arms above your head. Plié slightly, and position your hips directly under theirs.

Using your pelvis as leverage, straighten the knees to extend up and out, and curve forward to a comfortable placement where you have the full weight of their body stretched over your back (their feet are now off the ground).

In this position, you alternate pushing up on your lower back and your upper back, and one side and then the other, and whatever else feels comfortable to you.

This exercise is twofold, and is partially meant as a stretch for you using the weight of your partner's body as passive resistance—they are just along for the ride. Meanwhile the lifted partner reaps the benefits of dead weight responding to your movement, as little waves of motion rock them in the tension and release of your stretches. Incidentally, you have just also lifted their full weight off the ground, supporting them primarily by your skeletal structure.

Slowly lower their feet to the ground and, straightening your back, release their wrists.

Switch roles.

Exercise 1: a variation

This exercise can also be conducted on the floor by positioning yourself on the floor on all fours. Your partner then drapes themselves over your back, and you push up on their dead weight as before.

The advantage is that you are able to easily support their weight from this sturdy "quatro-pod" position, and for anyone uncomfortable with the idea of supporting weight, this is a good starting place. The disadvantage is that you do not yet have the experience of weight support in a standing position.

Exercise 2: back over back

As in the last exercise, you will be lifting the full weight of your partner off the ground, but this time back to back, focusing more specifically on using your pelvis as leverage.

Stand back to back with your partner, hands again holding their wrists above your head. Bend your knees so that again, your pelvis is slightly below theirs. Using your pelvis as leverage, tuck under theirs and simultaneously stretch their arms up and over as you bend in a gently curve forward.

The consistent stretch of the arms helps to elongate the spine as their feet leave the ground.

Again, find a comfortable final position for yourself. You can rest your hands on your thighs once their weight is comfortably balanced over your back. Do not hesitate to re-position them if you have found the initial leverage to be difficult or the final position hard to maintain. This weight-taking should be almost effortless.

It is useful to think of the stretch as "up and over" and not merely bent forward. Too deep a plié or curving too far forward will position their weight disproportionately over yours—your partner will feel top-heavy and your quads will work over-time. You are aiming to distribute their weight equally over your back, using your strong pelvic girdle as the initial leverage and as the center balance-point of their weight. Every body fits differently with every other body, so adjust your initial back-to-back position as needed, taking their center of gravity into consideration—a woman's center of gravity tends to be in the hips, and a man's is higher, usually in the chest. Your able skeleton has done the job; the secret of dead weight manipulation lies in finding the correct balance between your two bodies, and using your skeleton to initiate and support the lift.

As you support their entire weight, your partner is able to release into the stretch, opening space between vertebrae and in the shoulders. Your partner breathes deeply out (a little difficult in this position) and actively imagines release into this curve. Release your partner slowly, lowering their entire elongated body, feet finally touching the ground.

Switch places.

Exercise 3: waterfall preparation

Sit squatting back to back with your partner, and hook elbows. Leaning against each other's backs, come up to standing.

Go back down to sitting, still in contact with each other.

Repeat this a few times adjusting distance as needed between your two bodies (feet as close to your partner's as possible) and keeping the mutual pressure back to back. Unhook elbows and allow the balance to come through the pressure in your back.

Exercise 4: waterfall

Your goal is to go from standing to sitting using each other's weight, but this time to also transfer weight back and forth in the descent.

Begin standing back to back, as close as possible and, as before, push against your partner's back as you descend. Simultaneously open your arms to the side and arch your chest backwards—your partner will be obliged to counter your movement, bending forward. Switch postions as you continue your downward journey. Alternate weight forward and backward until you reach your sitting position. You have, like a waterfall, transferred weight in stages during your continuous flow downwards (p. 104).

Do the same thing, in reverse, ending in your original standing position.

Very quickly you will find that careful listening to your partner's movement and a mutual consciousness of this shifting weight is the only way to succeed. Use your arms opening out to the sides to help your equilibrium.

Repeat the waterfall several times with your partner, until you have succeeded in a full descent and ascent, with at least three shifts of weight in each direction.

Switch partners.

Be aware that again the difference in physical structure of your new partner (height, mass, flexibility, and weight—note that I did not mention strength) will make a difference in how you need to counterbalance them in order to keep equilibrium. Make sure that you actually give them some of your weight—we can all cheat and rise up and descend on our own applying little or no pressure to our partner's back, but what is the point? Experiment. You will probably lose balance, but that is the only way to find the correct dosage of weight to give and take with this particular partner.

Exercise 5: waterfall spiral

This is the same exercise, but now in three dimensions.

Again, start standing with your partner. As you begin your descent, opening your arms and arching your chest back, give yourself the option to twist slightly to the side. The sideways nuance allows you to shift weight support to different parts of your back, and you really get the feeling of a downward spiral in this variation. Continue with several shifts of weight exchange to reach sitting.

Rise up, and switch partners.

This ultimate waterfall is pleasant to execute and beautiful to watch. It takes advantage of multiple areas of weight support in the back, allowing the spine to undulate as the body twists and the arms to open in three-dimensional counterbalance.

The waterfall exercise emphasizes both weight giving and taking in a continuously shifting counterbalance. It is an excellent segue into Group 3 and 4 exercises of mutual support.

Group 3 exercises: floor support

ABOUT SAFETY AND GOOD SENSE

As good sense tells us, all of our partnering exercises need to be executed in an open space, on an even, friendly surface—a sprung dance floor is optimum, a cement floor is the worst; and while a green lawn may be enticingly soft, it is hazardously uneven. Work sensibly where you are able. Rolls in Group 3 are often executed on a tatami mat in martial arts classes, but without this luxury you can still easily run the sequence wearing a sweatshirt and sweatpants for extra padding. (Although I once had an aikido master teacher tell me that the best way to learn aikido rolls was on a cement floor—after a few bruises you quickly learn to avoid anything other than perfect placement. I opt for a gentler education.) Use padding as needed, find the best available surface, and work actively and intelligently. Throwing yourself thoughtlessly into movement is not brave—it is stupid. Rather follow the outlined sequence (exercises are ordered in a certain sequence on purpose), listen to physical cues, and work with a partner with whom you are comfortable. In exercises where any fear arises, work with a third person spotting until you are secure in the movement. In any case, in all of the two-person contact improvisation exercises, there is a shared responsibility for weight and momentum. You are not alone; and this consciousness engenders pleasure in shared execution and confidence in shared exploration.

You are ready for the next step.

Exercise 1: baby roll

The baby roll is a solo exploration of your weight against the floor.

Sit with a curved back, and grasp your feet allowing your knees to fall out to the sides (much like the butterfly exercise from the warm-up).

Your goal is to roll as a perfect ball in a circle. Making sure there is clear space in a circular area behind you, rock onto your right knee (using your elbow as an additional surface if you want). Roll onto your shoulder, across your upper back, and onto the opposite knee and elbow and finally onto your pelvis as you find yourself sitting back in your original position. Take a few consecutive rolls, letting momentum carry you.

Roll in the opposite direction.

It will take a little practice to find the softest, easiest way to roll, keeping the motion continuous without stopping on your back. Make sure that your pelvis stays lifted off the ground when you roll through your upper back, and that you cushion each point of contact by a gradual shift of rolling weight.

Now that you understand the trajectory, open your hands, arms still curved, as if you are holding a giant beach ball. You will also notice that your back and pelvis are curved in a second beach-ball position. Open your feet slightly to a comfortable position about 6 inches/15 cm apart, keeping your knees comfortably open to the sides.

Your goal is to make yourself as round as possible, and to let your wise body take the impact of the floor in progressive stages, becoming the optimum rolling surface. Similar to the closed baby roll, use your curved right arm to contact the floor through your wrist and knee, rolling onto your elbow, shoulder, and across your upper back and down the left shoulder, elbow, knee, and wrist, rocking back onto your pelvis (p. 108). This is actually an easier roll for many people; it just depends on the initial shape of your body and careful "round" positioning. Repeat it one direction and then the other, stopping if you get too dizzy.

These rolls are reminiscent of a baby in a crib happily playing with the momentum of their own weight. As adults our baby fat is long gone, so your goal is to ease your way without thumping or bumping. Baby rolls are a playful and useful way of introducing your body to easy maneuverability on the floor using many unexpected surfaces of your body for locomotion.

Exercise 2: spine roll-down

Like the baby roll, in the spine roll-down we look for the most economical way for you to propel your body against the friendly floor. But this time, your goal is to move from standing to lying on the ground.

Start standing, center of gravity and weight slightly forward on the front leg. Slide the other leg back a large step and bend the knees, leaning forward with your torso and arms to counterbalance your pelvis reaching back to sit.

When your pelvis sits (with torso naturally still counterbalancing forward), legs are on the ground with one knee bent.

Unravel your spine (remember all those spine undulations in warm-up), place your stretched arms last on the ground above your head, back of the hand gently slapping the ground (p. 110).

Stand up any way you would like, and repeat the movement again, this time moving the other foot back to initiate the roll-down.

There is no mystery about this movement—you are basically gradually lowering your pelvis to the floor, and unrolling the spine against the ground after that. The key is to lean substantially forward as you move your foot back—almost in a full lunge. The more you step back, the more you lean forward, and the closer the floor is as your knees bend. Also key is use of the arm above the head at the end of the movement. In a mild version of a martial art break-fall (breaking the fall with a slap on the ground to absorb some of the momentum of impact), this slap both distributes the extended weight more evenly and it creates a final resting place for your energy, avoiding the head hitting the ground. The continuousness of the action, and the use of counterbalanced gravity (why fight it?) in your descent, is the reason that this simple roll-down is one of the most economical ways to take full body weight from standing to lying on the ground. Martial artists and stage combatants are in on the secret and have used variations of this movement for many years.

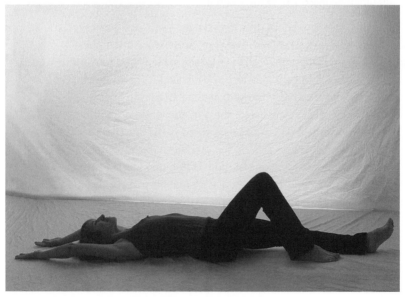

Exercise 3: push me/pull you

This is basically the same movement as in the spine roll-down, except
that this time you are executing it with a partner.

Stand facing your partner and hold each other's right wrists. Slide
the foot closest to them (the right) back behind you, and roll down
as in the previous exercise, pulling them along for the ride. Your
partner is pulled forward a few steps by your weight and momentum
as you roll to the floor.

You begin to curve your upper back forward to stand and your partner simultaneously steps backwards a few steps, counterbalancing your weight to "help" you to stand.

As soon as you have rolled back up your spine onto your legs, they roll down, pulling you forward this time, in their momentum down.

And you are ready to repeat push me/pull you.

There are several details to remember in the execution of this enjoyable weight exchange. For stabilization in the descent, it is important to take the foot closest to your partner backwards. There is a tendency while descending to bend only one knee (which makes your weight heavy for your partner). Bend both knees slightly. The continuous tension in your right arms is critical for smooth action. Once you are down on the ground and beginning to curve up, your partner needs to step backward fearlessly, trusting in the combination of your weight opposing their descent, and their own ability to unroll the spine against the ground. Remember the final extension of arm above the head—it is actually a great help in progressively distributing the weight and makes it easier for your partner to guide you to the ground. Clearly the continuous counterbalance of the two opposing bodies is key to an easeful exchange.

Repeat six or so exchanges until you feel confident in the flow.

Switch partners.

As in all mutual weight exchange exercises, a new partner demands new adjustments (how much weight to give, how deep to bend your knees and how much to lean back in counterbalance). Take care of your partner—the point is not to descend, the point is to continuously balance the weight between you.

Exercise 4: push me/pull you see-saw

This variation is composed of exactly the same action as push me/pull you, but reduces your motion forward and backward to one large step.

Once you are comfortable with the push me/pull you exchange, try the same exercise with your left foot fixed in place. The mutual lowering/descending of your partner demands a lunge forward on the foot closest to your partner (your right foot). And their ascent demands a lunge backwards using the same foot. The left foot is fixed in place, it is not going anywhere.

Repeat this a few times, noting the complicit nature of the opposition with your partner.

The see-saw effect is weight exchange at its most obvious, and is easier for some people to execute than the first push me/pull you. By getting rid of the fast little steps forward and backward, the emphasis shifts from being pulled along by momentum to a simple, controlled exchange of weight. Both exercises are valuable and playful examples of mutual weight support using the floor.

Exercise 5 (optional): aikido roll prep

This exercise builds on Exercise 2, and is a solo exercise in rising and falling to the ground with a minimum amount of muscling.

Start on one knee, and roll down your spine as before.

The only difference is that this time you turn out as you descend, allowing the knee to fall out to the side as the back rolls down.

Let the momentum of the roll continue so that your legs naturally go back into an outstretched plough, feet touching the ground behind your head.

Roll back up, placing one knee under you (turned out), and the other placed in a sturdy kneeling position.

Roll up and down a few times, and become familiar with this easy use of momentum.

Do the same and use the momentum of the pelvis descending and the spine unraveling to propel you to standing. Transfer weight onto the forward leg, and make sure to pass through the stable triangular position of kneeling (torso inclined forward) on your way up to standing. You will arrive with one leg behind the other, weight naturally transferred onto the forward leg. As in the spine roll-down, take the energy and weight forward and up, leaning your torso into the ascent from kneeling to standing.

From standing, simply slide one foot backward to begin the descent as before, but this time remember to pass through the triangular kneeling position before lowering your pelvis and unrolling your spine.

The gradual transition of weight to standing is economical, elegant, and eventually effortless. Continued practice will make the inevitable clunking to the ground disappear, but you will probably want to wear a thick sweatshirt and sweatpants for padding in the first few sessions of practice until your body finds its correct balance.

Exercise 6: body surfing—solo preparation

Lie full length on the ground on your back. Your goal is to roll across the room using your pelvis as locomotion.

Cross your right bent knee as far as possible over your left leg (as in the spine twist in the warm-up), and continue the movement, rolling onto your stomach dragging your torso behind in a comfortable twisting roll of your entire body. Once you have rolled onto your stomach, do not let the motion stop, but continue to roll with the pelvis leading (you will probably need to cross the left leg over the right now and allow this new weight to turn the rest of the body over in a continuing twisting roll). Keep going in the same trajectory across the room. You will probably find that you cannot continue to roll in a straight line, and are curving as you roll. That is normal, just keep going and enjoy the stretch of your spine in the process. Do not worry about the placement of your arms, they can drag along for the ride next to your body (sometimes getting rolled over in the process) or you can extend them above your head as your roll.

Do the same thing with the chest leading this twisting roll across the room. This time your arms will initiate the movement and your pelvis will drag behind as dead weight.

Alternate. A half roll onto your stomach, pelvis leading, is followed by a half roll onto your back, chest leading. You will find that this feels far more natural, and like the other two twist/rolls can be a luxurious stretch of the upper and lower back. It is also the most economical way to roll lengthwise across the floor.

Now you are ready to body surf, and to begin you are the rolling wave.

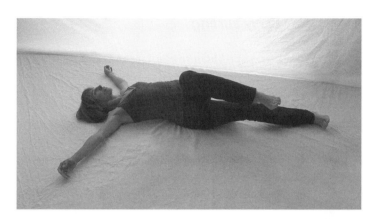

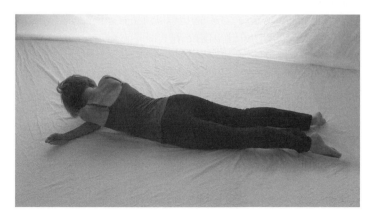

Exercise 7: body surfing

Work with a partner who is about your weight and height. Lie on the ground lengthwise on your back. Your partner places themselves stomach down, arms outstretched across your torso.

Like superman, their arms are pointed in the direction they will travel, and your immediate goal is to roll, propelling them toward their destination. Your mutual goal is to reach the end of the room, alternating roles of surfer and waves.

Using their hands to initiate the movement, your partner "walks" their body forward as you begin rolling, a churning wave. They "ride the wave" propelled forward by the momentum of your roll. When they have finished their ride (and it goes fast), you quickly change places and roles. You place your arms on level with their hips and are propelled forward as they roll. Once both partners are rolling, you will find it easier to maintain momentum, even in the quick changing of roles.

Well-matched partners and correct initial placement makes this task a mere question of logistics. Good body surfing partners listen well to each other, co-ordinating their mutual momentum, and enjoying the sensation of a day in the surf. The surfer maintains an extended line of trajectory and, by holding perfect zero, makes themselves light and maneuverable. The surfer also lends a hand as needed, walking their body forward whenever rolling becomes cumbersome (especially at the beginning of the wave). We notice the importance of sustained alignment, and the importance of a common center of gravity to facilitate weight manipulation. In the exercises in Group 3, we have gone from simple weight support to active and alternating manipulation of rolling weight. This interdependence is imperative for the standing weight exercises in Group 4.

Group 4 exercises: lifts

The golden rule for lifts is that the person lifted is responsible for holding their own weight. No matter how strong your partner, if you are not correctly "holding" your body in a strong and aligned perfect zero, they will be unable to successfully manipulate your weight. Also of importance is finding the mutual center of balance, because from this pivot point all action can be initiated and controlled.

Exercise 1: trust fall/rocking

Stand directly behind your partner, and place your hands just below their shoulder blades. Your partner stands in perfect zero, reminding themselves of the small lift around the solar plexus necessary for maintaining correct alignment. Lean the full weight of their body into your supporting hands, as they remain elongated and held in this straight line.

Rock them back to standing, always maintaining contact with your hands on their back. Rock them back and forth a few times,

continuing to maintain the contact, and inclining your body in opposition to theirs in order to counter their weight with your full body as opposed to using just your arms.

Many people are afraid to relinquish their full standing weight to a partner (particularly an unseen partner, stationed behind them). This self-protection is understandably human, but it is not particularly useful for the successful contact practitioner. Practice of this exercise, leaning the partner back in the smallest possible incline, establishes necessary trust and gives the partner experience in "holding" themselves while being manipulated by someone else. There are several keys to successful execution for both partners:

The person being rocked needs to absolutely maintain a perfect zero without breaking alignment—there is a tendency to bow the stomach out in order to keep control.

Remind yourself instead to keep the lift around your solar plexus, holding your aligned position with the minimum amount of tension necessary. Smile, and breathe. Like a baton, it is easiest to manipulate weight that is progressively extended and reliably rigid. Breaking or bowing the spine actually makes it harder for the lifter—who is now obliged to deal with the uneconomical weight of a misaligned spine.

As the lifter, you need to remember the ever-useful concept of counterbalance. Place one foot behind the other in a small lunge, and oppose their inclined weight. As a general rule of thumb, counterbalance forward as much as they lean backward. The perfect balance point between your bodies is a perfectly comfortable place of support where you do very little work with your muscles and instead rely on structural opposition.

Experiment rocking your partner backward a little further and note how your position changes in exact proportion to theirs. Make a small, very small, experiment with a forewarned partner, and take your hands off their shoulders for a brief moment, allowing their weight to fall into your hands before you catch it, and note how much heavier they become with the momentum of the brief free-fall. *Continuously supported, gradually changing weight is lighter and easier to manipulate.*

Change roles.

Steve Paxton (the originator of contact improvisation) once said to treat your partner as if they were a wild animal that you did not want to scare. It is very important to make your partner feel safe, so keep your hands in close contact in these early stages of trust. It is equally important for them to keep their eyes open, and to not hold their breath.

Exercise 2: trust fall/skeleton

This exercise builds on the previous trust fall, but this time you catch your partner's weight supporting with different parts of your skeleton.

Stand behind your partner as before, and now guide them back, this time leaning their upper back onto your shoulder.

Experiment to find the most stable point of support, and then experiment lowering them by bending your knees and/or walking back a few small steps (always keeping in mind the principle of counterbalance and opposition of your weight to theirs). Feel free to use your hands as additional support or to re-position them at anytime that it feels awkward. If they begin to feel heavy, you have gone too far. Come back and try again.

Try using an unexpected part of your body to support them (chest, middle back, feet, and head have all been successfully used). Your reliable skeleton is now the structural support for their weight, and successful variations rely on using strong points of skeletal support at a good angle of counterbalance to your advantage.

Exercise 3: dead chicken

Stand side by side with your partner and put your arms around each other's waist.

Step in front of them, thrusting your right hip in front of theirs, and with a small plié using your right hip as leverage, lift their dead weight onto your hip/lower back (they will most likely be placed on an angle somewhere between the two).

The movement should be easy to do and holding this position of support should be effortless—you are not using your will power or even primarily using your muscles. You are using a very reliable part of your skeletal structure to hold them. Experiment. The exact common point of balance will vary depending on the height, weight and mass of your two bodies together, so explore placement by

plié-ing more or less, and shifting them more onto the back and less onto the hip.

Once you feel you have found correctly balanced placement, take your arms away, and see if they are stable. You will know very quickly if you need further adjustments.

Try walking with your partner (you can put your arm back for moral support). Your walk will probably feel more like a lurch as your off-center hip continues balancing their weight.

Lower their feet to the ground, and switch roles.

In this exercise, your partner is released, limp weight easily supported by your skeleton. This is an exception to the golden rule of weight support, and in this case the lifter is responsible for controlling the leveraging hip and positioning the dead weight on an easy point of balance.

Exercise 4: solo flower/flying

This solo exercise is a preparation for the flying chicken exercise.

Lie on your stomach on the ground. In an easy five count, slowly "blossom" lifting arms and legs and head progressively into a gentle arch. Hit your maximum, and slowly lower down in a five count.

Repeat this three times, making sure to progressively expand into full flying/blossoming.

Exercise 5: flying chicken

This is an exhilarating balance exercise. For moral support more than for safety, you may want to work in trios, alternating one person as spotter.

Take your partner, as before, into a perfectly balanced dead chicken lift. Continuing to hold onto them, your partner now goes from dead chicken to flying chicken, arms opening to the front or to the sides of their fully arched body.

You may need to slightly readjust to their new weight. You will find them lighter, but less stable, as their pelvis balances on your lower back/hip.

Swing their feet to the ground, and switch roles.

You will find that the baton-like rigidity of their progressively distributed weight makes them easy to maneuver and manipulate. Flying chicken is the archetype of many lifts relying on skeletal support.

After repeating flying chicken several times with both partners, explore some small shifts of weight. Small changes in the lifter's

support can drastically shift the position of the person being lifted. When lifted, be ready and willing to adjust or to swing down to your feet. The willing body can swing from a side hip lift to the other hip, to across the back (remember the jitterbug?). Explore these variations with a little momentum only when comfortably secure— legs can bend as needed, but the back continues to be arched and the body held.

These experiments can be great fun, but both partners need to stay attentive to each other and always find the mutual point of gravity and balance. Remember, your partner is a wild animal that you do not want to scare. Err on the side of safety.

ABOUT PHYSICAL PROXIMITY

As we have seen in previous exercises, lifts demand a unified momentum, the willingness and ability of the liftee to hold their own weight, and a common center of balance and gravity. What all this boils down to is that the two partners must be in very close proximity to each other for the lifts to be safe. Dancers accustomed to physicalizing these precepts will have no problem accepting the obvious close contact. The strong physical actor also needs to relinquish norms concerning acceptable social distance. As a working actor, you pride yourself on self-knowledge and that includes an acceptance of your body's size and weight. It also includes respect for yourself and for your partner in any skill-oriented exercise, and most especially in exercises of mutual balance and weight where safety is a concern. A partner who takes a modest distance in a supporting lift that demands a common center of gravity is actually putting both partners at risk. Work with a partner with whom you are comfortable, and acknowledge the common task you are engaged in. Be grateful for their participation, because without them you would be unable to proceed. In martial arts classes we often bow to our partners at the end of practice, and in the movement studio we often thank partners at the end of a contact improvisation session. We all learn from each other, and are unable to execute these movements without our partner's active participation. We are privileged to work with them.

Exercise 6: koala bear

The koala is a lift that has always amazed with its unexpected ability to work for different body types and sizes. Execution relies on establishing a common center of gravity that is not overwhelmed by an overly forceful initiation of the lift. In this case it is almost entirely the responsibility of the partner being lifted to maintain the safety of both. As in the flying chicken, this exercise is best introduced to a group of three—alternating lifter, liftee, and spotter. Initially, partners of similar weight should work together, or the lifter should be the larger of the two.

Stand facing your partner. The partner (or base) stands in a stable, small second position, feet shoulder width apart, knees slightly bent. The base is now prepared for you to jump to final position, and is solidly grounded, weight ever so slightly leaning forward.

Place your forearms on your partner's shoulders, your hands joined behind their neck. Your goal is to push directly down, and simultaneously spring to position holding your bent knees on their torso, like a koala on a tree.

Critical to the success of this simple lift (really a solo effort with a complicit partner) is pressure down on your forearms (*not* pulling forward on their neck), a straight lifted back, and a close approach. If you stand back from your partner and jump forward onto them, you bowl them backward with your momentum. Likewise if you jump up high and land heavily grabbing them around the neck, you pull them forward off-balance.

So stand close to your partner (you can even be French and kiss them on both cheeks—you should be *that* close). Pushing straight down on their shoulders, initiate your mount with a tiny jump straight up, grabbing them with your knees on either side of their waist. Keep your back straight and held high. (The only complaint your partner should have concerns the locked grip of your strong legs.) If you have pulled your partner forward or backward, adjust

your momentum and try again. The third person as spotter, meanwhile, stations themselves to the side, ready to help stabilize if needed.

Switch roles, again making sure in these initial forays that the base is of equal size or larger than the person lifted.

A common error in the koala is for the person being lifted to let their pelvis sag, thereby lowering their center of weight and making themselves heavy, pulling their partner forward. It is important to keep the stomach and lower back lifted, and to imagine a common center of gravity with your partner. A common lifted center of gravity will always feel light and manageable even if there is actually considerable weight.

When you are comfortable with the practical logistics of this lift, you can experiment with skillful partners of varying sizes.

Exercise 7: straight-leg koala

This is exactly the same exercise, but instead of bent knees, you will be attaching to the tree with straight legs.

As in the previous exercise, stand facing your partner, forearms resting on their shoulders, prepared to find the common center of gravity between you and your tree in a perfect mount. As you jump up, extend your legs straight out in front of you. The koala is now sitting, but the principle of gripping with the legs around the waist and holding up the lower back remains the same.

Exercise 8: kama sutra lift

Much like its namesake, this exercise explores physical positioning of partners, but this time the goal is an exploration of dance lifts of mutual balance.

Stand facing your partner (as in the koala) but this time your partner is in a large second position plié, and instead of jumping to place, simply wrap your legs around their supporting thighs (p. 132).

This is really a weight and balance exploration that begins in this very stable and solid position. Begin moving away from your mutual center of gravity by leaning backward, arching your back. Your partner will counterbalance by mirroring you.

Explore how far this backbend can take you as your partner continues to maintain opposition from a sturdy second position.

Arms and hands will continue to shift grasp as you continue exploring—always locked in stable contact with your partner. Wrapping feet around your partner's back or legs is yet another option for stabilization (p. 132).

Your partner is obliged to always counterbalance your weight in these forays, leaning back in direct proportion to you.

Move back to the common center of gravity and this time explore by moving *around* it—for instance shifting your weight to sit on one of your partner's thighs or hips.

Your partner will not move from base position, but will need to be attentive to your movement cues, bending knees or leaning in opposition as they seek the perfect counterbalance. You must also remain sensitive to them, only moving in subtle weight shifts.

Experiment in continued positioning on the back, or as we saw in the flying chicken jitterbugging reference, even higher up around the waistline.

The goal is simply to play—using your partner as a sturdy but flexible jungle gym that you do not want to throw off-balance. Mutual responsiveness to weight shifts is especially obvious in the kama sutra lift. You can move away from the center of common gravity, or around it, but either way only sensitive counterbalancing by both partners will allow for any freedom of movement.

The variables in this exercise have grown—principles of weight exchange and balance are used to create positions only possible between your two bodies. Explore this exercise until comfortably creative. Congratulations—you are now reaching a point of physical freedom and skill that is conducive for contact improvisation.

CHAPTER 5

Contact Improvisation

Contact improvisation is a dance improvisation form based on energy and weight exchange, incorporating elements of aikido, jitter-bugging, child's play, and tumbling. Creator Steve Paxton defines it as "the ideal of active, reflexive, harmonic, spontaneous, mutual forms." Exploding into popularity with modern dancers in the 1970s, contact "jams" sprang up in dance studios and church basements all over the USA, inviting dancers, friends of dancers, and their children to participate.

The sophisticated and technically trained professional brought the tools of the trade to the contact floor, while the novice brought energy and willingness, but what was prized in both was instinctive movement, and playfulness. Rules went out the window as spontaneity of discovery was stressed in partnering, and new forms were created to support physical contact. These forms were mostly exercises taken from other movement disciplines to help partners give and take weight.

The joyous and intimate quality of this improvisatory dance form has remained popular, and practice is now also widespread in Europe both as a dance technique and as a social interaction. Contact improvisation remains an exceptional tool for the strong physical actor, though our goals are a little different. We take the basic premise of energy and weight partnering and then adapt it for an actor's skills and goals: relaxed, instinctive responses to a partner's motion, and a courageous "intimacy." The alert practitioner takes these physical skills from the contact dance floor into the rehearsal room, and in a seamless interplay of word, gesture, and motion, actors are driven by the content and rhythm of the text and by the subtext of the scene. Physical intimacy is compelling to the voyeuristic audience, and can be perceived even between actors sitting on separate sides of a room. Intimacy, in this case, does not necessarily imply sexuality, but alludes to a physical awareness and responsiveness that is only slightly heightened from the everyday.

How do we create this charged atmosphere, and easy partnership for the non-dancer?

You are almost there.

In warm-up (Chapter 1) you prepared the body in stretch, strength, and alignment exercises. Spatial orientation and dynamic awareness of the group was explored in Chapter 2, and principles of energy exchange, isolated movement, and counterbalance were developed through mime exercises (Chapter 3). Partnering techniques for giving and supporting weight with confidence were practiced in Chapter 4.

You are now ready to take on the actor's contact improvisation. Size, age, and technical limitations do not pose boundaries, because unlike dance improvisation, physical prowess and presentational form is not our goal; rather, we are aiming for an evolving, sensitive communication with the other. The spatial awareness and partnering tools gained from the preceding chapters allow you to respond instinctively and safely in physical interaction. The actor engaged in a contact improvisation is inevitably compelling, and incidentally often graceful, balanced, harmonious, and full of surprises.

You are ready to begin.

Preliminary improvisation

The fying saucer and trading fours improvisations are space and causality exercises. Trading fours is the perfect segue into full contact for the equipped physical actor. The flying saucer improvisation takes us there.

Exercise 1: flying saucer improvisation (solo)

Stand with lots of space around you. Imagine a surface parallel to you (the size of a small window), and push against it with your hands. It resists, pushing you back. Push again, and again it pushes back. The third time that you push, slightly tilt the surface—there is no resistance! You almost fall with the unexpected speed and flow, following the trajectory of the flying saucer, spinning, swooping, and changing direction with each small tilt of the surface in a new direction.

You don't impose or create— you follow the trajectory of the energy. This is very important.

Watch a few practitioners, and explore again this sensation of being guided through space by an energy flow.

You are now ready to trade fours.

Exercise 2: trading fours

Trading fours (a dancer's count of four) is productive for both the novice and experienced contactor. This improvisation ends many technique sessions, and is always positively influenced by the work that has come before.

Your partner takes a position in space (*any* position, from standing with extended arms to crouching on the ground). Your job is to complement that shape, making a single sculpture of your two bodies. You have a count of four to move into a responding position:

Four for nothing, two, three, four.

Go.

As soon as you hit your final position on four, your partner responds to you in the following four, and this alternating call and response of trading fours, has begun. The count and dialogue are continuous.

Explore positive and negative space in your positioning (those positions you create and the area surrounding your body). Think of your body as a pliable sculpture, and note how your two positions interact in positive and negative space. Relish the pleasure of participatory form. It is also important to initially consider the energy with which your partner moves into their position. One novice practitioner thought this exercise was called "trading force" and he was also correct. Take the force and flow of the partner's motion and respond to it. If the final trajectory of their movement is a full lunge with extended arm and hand, your goal is not to mirror them, or copy them, but to let the extended energy of that hand initiate your next count of four. As we have seen in previous exercises, action demands reaction. Their hand may be extended toward your shoulder, and so your shoulder is initial recipient of their force. A directed line of energy can throw you backwards in response, or your body can take that same energy into a turn or spiral. Your clever body counterbalanced within itself will automatically follow-through.

So let it.

Thank your partner and switch. Experience the completely different energy of your new partner—new ways of moving will emerge with this unique individual. Trading fours changes with each partner, and can change with each day. The sky is the limit within the structural boundaries of sensitive partnering.

Thank this partner and switch again. But before you do, it is often useful to watch one pair who are listening well. Watching an actively engaged couple improvise before switching again is exciting and usually informative. You can literally see what works and what does not.

Work with several different partners, three to five in a session is plenty, and always thank them when you are done.

Exercise 2: variations

Use music

Using music (with an obvious and consistent beat) can free the mind if you are over-analyzing, but it can also dictate movement—so do not simply dance. Let the music inform your movement and remember that the nuance of movement given by your partner is the dictating force.

Focus on causality

Although energy exchange is always a part of the work, specifically focusing on it within a session can really help instill the concept in your body. Similar to the isolation energy toss in the mime chapter, trading fours with a focus on causality gives each action at the end of your count of four a reaction at the beginning of your partner's four count—a virtual ping-pong match.

With isolations

Find a single isolation or body part (shoulders, hips, heads, for example) and continue trading fours, both partners using this general focus. You are free to move your entire body, but your exchange will primarily focus on this isolation.

At a distance

Start across the room from your partner, responding to their motion from afar. Movements may get smaller, subtler—that is fine.

Move toward your partner if you have not already. Note the difference. All variations of shape and motion, large and small, touching or not, are acceptable.

Hands touching

This is, in fact, a key exercise toward moving into contact improvisation and should only be done after trading fours is comfortably established with the normal count. When you are in consistent contact, you naturally pull your partner along in your trajectory. Try a trading fours touching using hands. You can switch hands, break away and rejoin hands, or use both hands at will: let the trajectory of the motion tell you what to do. You will find that the count muddies— there is no longer a clear distinction of who is moving and who is frozen. Instead, there are two participating bodies following through the line of action. Continue to trade initiating the motion, but allow your partner's action to literally pull you along and do not worry about an exact count of four. No longer dictated by an external count, the "stop" is now dictated by the flow of the movement itself reaching its logical conclusion before starting up again. Just follow the river.

Contact improvisation

Take the inevitable contact of joined hands pushing and pulling pliant bodies and let go of the hands, allowing the energy between you and your partner to continue to dictate your motion. Hands are no longer a focus; touching or not depends on the movement that arises between you. Weight (your own with the floor or balanced with your partner) is also a playful consideration in the exchange. Early contact sessions are easiest without mutual weight—so work now without exchanging weight with your partner, focusing instead on the transference of energy following the line of motion in your new-found freedom without counts. Be alert to the counterbalance of weight within your own body as it responds effortlessly to theirs.

Stand back to back with your partner and breathe. Feel their back against yours and respond to the tiny cues of pressure from their ribs. Spend a little minute in mutual motion dictated by your breath, and let this action initiate your next contact session. You have already begun.

LOGISTICS OF CONTACT SESSIONS

A contact session begins with one of many possible set-ups (back to back, focus on breath is only one) and lasts as long as is beneficial—usually three to five minutes. It is useful to watch two contactors and share observations or perceptions of their work before changing partners for the next session. Honesty of movement and a true connection is basically what we are after. Three to six changes of partners in a group session is typical.

Switch partners.

Stand back to back with your partner, and spin around three times. Freeze! Your position now in relationship to his or her position initiates the session.

Begin.

The beauty and freedom of contact improvisation is that there is no right or wrong instinctive movement—there is only honestly following through the established line of energy. The only wrong you can do is to force the action.

You are not here to entertain us, or to dazzle us with your amazing acrobatic skill. You are here to communicate honestly with your partner: if you feel that you have nothing interesting to say, you are forcing the issue. Your "uninteresting" action, if it is honest, is enough. The relationship between you two is implied in the first moment. Follow through from your initial position where direction of energy and weight is already dictated—just follow the blueprint.

Switch partners, and work again, this time with music.

As in trading fours, consistency of beat is again useful but do not let it dictate. Music can give you permission to move without over-analyzing. Take this freedom from the music and allow it to inform your sensitivity to your partner—large movement can be just as good as small. Varying rhythm and playful follow-through is as valuable as slow, elongated sensuality. What remains consistent is an acute responsiveness and awareness to your partner in space.

Someone once said that the manners of the baroque era were the manners of the boudoir—intimate, attentive, and deeply personal. The same can be said of any good contact improvisation, even the joyous, rowdy acrobatic challenges. Especially in the acrobatic moments, you need to be intimately alert to shifts of energy, weight, and intention. Needless to say, this is a mutual awareness, with no one leading or following—just an endlessly changing and shifting of power, weight, and center of gravity.

How much fun is that?

If you have the opportunity to work with a group, watch an improvising pair, and share perceptions of qualities in their work (sensual, playful, combative are some that arise). Again, there is no right or wrong movement—but observations about work are useful. The potential pitfall here is to get "stuck" in one level of exchange, not allowing for the mandatory fluidity of change. If this happens,

forgive yourself and start up again. The endless creativity of the human spirit is a wonder to behold, and is an appropriate goal for the physical actor. Honesty is key. Do not push the river.

Start this time stretching backs with your partner—facing each other, hold wrists and lean away testing the counterbalanced weight between you.

You have already begun.

Take advantage of the unexpected points of contact you find with your partner. What actually happens is what is important, not what you thought was going to happen. The most wonderful, unexpected, and honest contact happens when you find yourself in unpredictable positions.

For example, in the middle of a contact session you might find yourself on your back on the floor, one bent knee hooked on your partner's shoulder. Allow that point of contact its full value. Your partner stands and slowly walks toward you, your hooked leg secure, and you slowly rise up into a shoulder stand, propelled by their action. When you reach a point of stasis, your attentive partner "testing" only as far as your body comfortably bends, you remain comfortably

suspended in air until a slight twist of your partner's shoulder releases your foot and you effortlessly roll down your spine and up to sitting. Your released weight triggers your partner to spin and stop suspended, facing your sitting body. Now their back leg leaves the ground, arms reach out in counterbalance as they cantilever forward. From sitting your arms rise in response, pelvis follows, and soon you are kneeling in a solid tripod position—your finger tips on your partner's, as you both gradually lean into the counterbalance of weight between your two bodies. The moment suspends, your partner's weight tilting extremely forward, you slowly standing, his (or her) weightless leg lowering in response. You are both now standing on two feet, touching fingertips shifting to wrists grasping, and you both lean away, tucking pelvis under, in a mutually supporting stretch.

This is a plausible moment of contact—partners have changed roles of support without conscious thought. There is an intimate negotiating in the mutual exploration of balance, and some of the principles of previous exercises have found themselves naturally coming into play. This is, after all, your vocabulary. Rhythms change, points of balance are carefully explored and released and you mutually take advantage of the moment that presented itself.

What to look for when observing

- Are both partners listening?
- Are they honestly responding or pushing the river?
- Is the use of energy, weight, and momentum safe?

This is very important—enthusiastic contactors new to lifts will sometimes go right to the edge of safety and then push past a point of balanced equilibrium to a dangerous potential disaster. Interestingly, the watching audience always senses the point where you are no longer safe, and they become uncomfortable watching. You have just defeated the point of a good contact improv session, not only for you and your partner, but also for anyone witnessing your work.

When the audience is concerned for your safety, they no longer vicariously follow the flow of the action, they are instead pulled away from the developing relationship and are focusing on external potential failure. Err on the side of safety—leave the triple flip to another day when it comes more naturally, and continue to take care of your partner.

- Are partners allowing the energy and flow to naturally come to a halt, and begin again?
- Are they allowing the energy to naturally change?

As in any good dialogue, you do not spend the entire time shouting in a predictable rhythm—make sure to allow change to happen. Repeated patterns can give the novice contactor a great deal of security, but eventually change needs to occur, and it will if you are listening.

Most essential for all contact is not just following what you *thought* was going to happen, but accepting the endless small turns in the road as new possibilities. The expected triple back-flip may become a spiraled descent and backwards roll. Do not look for the spectacular—accept instead what happens, and that dialogue with your unique partner will lead to surprising variations, plays of physical wit, and unexpected impossible actions.

BODY WISDOM

Aikido (literally translated "the way of harmonizing energy") is a martial art that explores complicit ways of leveraging and manipulating a partner's weight and momentum. Not surprisingly, contact creator Steve Paxton practiced aikido extensively, and defines it as one of the foundations of contact improvisation. Dr Mark Adachi is an aikido master and a chiropractor, a man whose life practice involves energy balance and structural flow. One day, during a professional visit to his LA office, he described the healing process of a frustrating injury.

"The hip is much stronger and more resilient. Your body is even storing energy now. It is preparing to work."

I replied that in that case, my body was far ahead of my intellect and emotions. He smiled and said, "Always."

The body is always ahead of the mind and heart. It is even now preparing for your next experience. Trust the information that it gives you.

Once your contact improvisation partnering becomes more natural, more exciting, and more vital, there are several other productive ways to initiate the work that you will want to experience.

Contact improvisation: milling 1

Begin by milling with the group (Chapter 2), and at a given moment allow your next milling relationship to become a contact improvisation, exchanging energy and weight without touching.

Move back into a general milling for a few minutes, and then segue at a given moment back into a contact improvisation, this time allowing for the mutual balance and weight exchange that can only come with touching.

Contact improvisation: milling 2

In another variation, begin once again with the group milling exercise, effortlessly changing partners within the group. Now begin a full contact improvisation with your most recent milling partner.

Move back into milling with the entire group, and continue to relate to your partner in space as you both mill. You will fall into normal milling relationships with others, but you simultaneously remain alert to your partner at a distance as your primary relationship.

Contact improvisation: tango

Start with a prescribed social dance step with a partner. The tango is particularly good, but any social dance with a consciousness of the action/reaction of partnering as you move as a duet through space will work.

Continue your dance steps, but let go of physical contact so that the energy between your two bodies is entirely guided through mutual responsiveness without touch.

Allow this action/reaction to deviate from the steps, and then allow it to develop into full contact not touching.

After establishing an energized, responsive exchange, add touching.

Contact improvisation: release

Work on a release exercise with your partner (and this can be as complicated as the Tanaka Min joint manipulation sequence or as simple as a head massage). Be aware of the weight in your body, and the willingness to relinquish control of manipulation to your partner.

Switch roles, be aware of your deepening, elongated breath as you relax, and of your partner's released weight.

Begin a contact improvisation alert to subtle shifts of relaxed weight.

Contact improvisation: eyes closed

Start with heads touching with your partner, and close your eyes.

Begin a full contact.

As with any movement with closed eyes, if you are ever unsure where your partner is in space, or wonder where the wall is, open your eyes, re-affirm positioning, and shut them again. This is not cheating, this is smart. Eyes-closed contact with heads usually results in a nuanced exchange as your unseen partner communicates in careful movement.

Contact improvisation: amoeba

As experienced in the exercise in Chapter 2, build a single-celled organism that moves in complicit group motion in the prescribed four count.

After executing successful ever-shifting changes of form as a group, splinter in partners and allow the amoeba-based complicit pairing to evolve into a full contact improvisation. The transformation of partnering structure is effortless.

Contact improvisation: twister

Stand elbow to elbow with your partner.

Add right knee to right knee.

Add nose to nose, and begin!

Follow the implied energy and weight in your position.

Everyone will interpret the commands slightly differently, and that is good! All beginnings will be personal, and complicit.

Contact improvisation: random beginning

This is probably the simplest, most economical and most natural way to begin a contact improvisation. Find a partner and . . .

Freeze!

From whatever random position you are in, continue the implied trajectory of energy and weight in your position while responding to the implied energy and weight of your partner's body in space.

You have already begun.

Now that you have engaged breath, weight, energy exchange, balance, and seamless exchange touching and not touching you are ready for the next step.

We add text.

Contact improvisation with text

How do we combine theatrical dialogue, driven as it is by conscious character goals, with the intuitive, intimate partnering of contact improvisation? The answer is simple: we productively interface text and contact by allowing the definition of scene work (implying thoughtful character analysis) and contact improv (implying organic, physical relating) to have separate integrity and then to influence each other. The intellectual breakdown of scene study is not discarded but, in fact, unconsciously informs the courageous contacting actor.

Several benefits occur from taking dialogue into contact improvisation: by simultaneously speaking and moving you free the body to respond effortlessly to the ever-important "other." Just this much is a revelation for some actors, who find that the act of speaking allows their body to effortlessly follow physical impulses. Kinetic partnering becomes an absent-minded process as the active mind concentrates on language, and allows the trained body instinctive responsiveness.

Beyond general ease in space with a partner, we also discover that physical responses in a contact with text are unconsciously influenced by power shifts between characters. Sub-text is made manifest in the improvisation, and as character desires are physicalized, emotionally connected blocking suggests itself. Taken one step further the heightened physical responsiveness of a good contact is shaped into character-appropriate movement. The impulses are the same, and the relationship remains viscerally connected, but the responses are manifest in realistic movement. A production that is highly stylized might revel in the complicit dance lift that emerges as appropriate behavior between dialoguing partners in a rowdy production of *A Midsummer Night's Dream*, but the same impulse in a realistic Chekhov scene might lead to a momentary, simultaneous turn toward each other, and then retreat back into everyday quotidian gestures of pouring tea and adjusting a pocket watch. Information about beats (where the actor resolves one thought and begins another) and masks (when can we uninhibitedly allow the true emotion to be revealed) is suggested with further contact exploration. The courageous physical actor uses the information gained to deepen character relationships and to inform blocking. While the director's vision of the story must be upheld and ultimately govern the staging, the actor working a scene in contact improvisation can bring honest physical responses back to rehearsal, and a wealth of new possibilities emerge.

We are reaching the ultimate goal of the contacting physical actor. You have already gained control over the body (through consistent stretch, strength, and alignment exercises) and have learned to navigate space with ease and presence. Articulated action has been incorporated in your gestures and motion, and all of these tools have come into play as kinetic responsiveness in partnering is explored.

Now we combine all these parts to make a whole and return the physical actor to the stage, and that implies the powerful context of a structured scene with text. The physical conditioning of the previous chapters is already a plus, a well-trained and expressive body is the responsibility of every actor. But we want to take the training further and move the contact improvisation into the rehearsal room.

Contact improvisation with dialogue

Choose a partner and freeze!

Begin contacting by allowing the position in which you find yourself, with all its implied weight and motion, to initiate the contact.

Once a good attentive, physical connection has been established (usually after two or three minutes of partnering), begin a conversation. You can talk about anything except what you are doing or feeling in the moment of contact. Do not stop to talk, and do not try to make eye contact. Just let the movement, driven by your energy and weight exchange continue with the text layered on top, almost as an after-thought of verbal communication.

Contact with conversation can have some hilarious results. Mundane and personal information emerges in this context of intimate physical trust. Little shared details emerge about preferred ice-cream flavors or one-up-manship telling stories about juvenile transgressions.

Simultaneously some actors experience an increased ability to unconsciously respond to their partner. The conscious mind is busy talking and allows the body to follow through lines of motion and weight without second-guessing itself.

Thank your partner, find a new partner and begin a new contact.

At a given moment begin talking.

After witnessing several contact improvisations with dialogue, you begin to see the way text evolves as punctuation to movements. And how the nature of the dialogue, excited and overlapping, or precise and controlled is often reflected in the movement. All of these tendencies are interesting to note, but unimportant to strive for at this point. What is important to strive for is a continued dis-interested simultaneity of action with your words. After the preparatory contact training in lifts and rolls, energy and weight, you need to allow your body to effortlessly respond to the subtle nuances of motion while speaking.

Now that you have experience speaking while contacting, leave your expectations at the door and bring an acting scene to the studio.

Contact improvisation with a scene

Hold the wrists of your partner and lean away, pelvis tucked under to stretch the lower backs. Shift the weight to stretch shoulders, and then straighten alternate legs to stretch hamstrings.

Pull up to standing to face your partner.

You have already begun.

Once the contact is well-established, begin speaking your text.

This is not a method for line memorization, so allow the dialogue to be delivered with intention. However, remain grounded in the movement—it is of primary importance in this exercise that the words flow on top of the action. How far along into the scene you are able to go is immaterial. Stop and get feedback if there are any observers, and talk to your partner about any discoveries.

What you find early in contact with scene work depends on the scene used. Since this exercise is intended as a rehearsal tool to enhance emotional/physical connection, it is most useful to work a scene you have already rehearsed in a more conventional manner. However, working with new text delivers spontaneous information about acting beats that can also be put to good use by the actor. Following are five examples of scenes worked with contact, and the immediate application to the stage. The movements described are taken verbatim from contact sessions between student actors in my movement studio.

The first scene is a flirtatious, romantic dialogue, followed by two extremes of scene choices—Shakespeare and Ibsen. We then explore two scenes taken from contemporary drama. It should be noted here that although working with a group has its benefits (rotating scene partners in example 1), contacting with a scene truly needs only two people—you and your partner.

One More Ride on the Merry-Go-Round

If you have the luxury of a working group, agree to memorize the same dialogue. Find a realistic scene where dialogue is exchanged between two people who are romantically attracted to each other, and are negotiating the boundaries of their relationship. Classic realism such as Odet's *Golden Boy*, or text from the screenplay of *How Harry Met Sally* are candidates, as are many contemporary romantic comedies.

Choose a partner, and begin walking, facing your partner. Eventually, someone here must walk backward, and responsive partners naturally shift the active and receptive roles. You can change direction as often as you want, just keep walking face to face.

Begin contacting.

Begin contacting with your scene.

The following is an example of a romantic comedy worked with contact.

Arnold Wesker's *One More Ride on the Merry-Go-Round*, Act 1, Scene 1.

Monica and Jason are two academics. They have recently become romantically involved, and are unsure how "serious" it might be.

Monica: Jason, you're a mess. You may have "found" yourself in bed but you've lost yourself in the world. Look at you! You need a shave.

Jason: You're turned on by my intellect, what need to shave?

Monica: Your bright brain may turn me on, but your grey stubble turns me right off again.

Jason: It's not grey!

Monica: Your beard's grey, your eyes are bloodshot, and tiny blood vessels have burst around your nose.

Jason: From the strain of it, the strain of it, goddammit!

Monica: Don't best with me, because I'm your match.

Jason: I'm not besting with you. "Besting" is getting the best and last word over a partner you don't really love, and you I love.

Here we go now in contact: Remember, do not stop moving to speak. The movement flows simultaneously with the text.

Monica is leaning over Jason's prone body, pushing one knee into his chest, and leaning comfortably on his other long leg, which is stretched up into the air. He holds onto the backs of her thighs. The mood is relaxed, playful, and intimate as Monica says,

> *"Jason, you're a mess."*

To better address him, she sinks slowly down to the ground while holding onto one of his legs for support, and he retaliates by slowly closing his legs to cut off her vision. As she continues to berate him, she is slowly tilting, pulled over by his leg.

> *"You may have 'found' yourself in bed but you've lost yourself in the world. Look at you!"*

He turns his back on her, gazing into the studio mirror, and she is pulled back up to sitting entwined in his leg, and following through the line of energy, ends by leaning against his elongated body. They both look in the mirror.

> *"You need a shave."*

He languorously rolls onto his stomach, and she body surfs the momentum of this roll, ending criss-crossed on his back. He lifts his head slightly, saying;

> *"You're turned on by my intellect, what need to shave?"*

She rolls off his body and onto her back, his limp arm pulled along. His hand has landed on her cheek, and he cradles her head affectionately. She touches his face saying,

"Your bright brain may turn me on, but your grey stubble turns me right off again."

The touch of her hand triggers him to turn his head away from her, and propped up by an arm he suddenly swivels all the way around, pinning her prone body to the ground as he says,

"It's not grey!"

He quickly rolls back the way he came, pulling her prone legs with him (he has cleverly wrapped his legs around hers and she cannot resist). He flips her around, and they both follow the momentum up to sitting,

"Your beard's grey, your eyes are bloodshot,"

She kicks her legs into the air and then rocks back up to her knees saying,

"And tiny blood vessels have burst around your nose."

Leaning into him, nose to nose.

He turns, annoyed now, and walks aggressively on his hands and knees toward her as she retreats backward sliding on her butt,

"From the strain of it, the strain of it, goddammit!"

She immediately rocks back up to defiant standing, as he counterbalances backward, now sitting on *his* butt,

"Don't best with me, because I'm your match."

"I'm not besting with you."

He rolls onto his back, placing his feet on her hips. He gently takes her hands, and unexpectedly lifts her into a flying position high above him, balanced on his feet as he says,

"'Besting' is getting the best and last word over a partner you don't really love,"

She is suspended in the air as he speaks and, as he continues, he slowly bends his knees, lowering her closer to his body with each word.

"And you I love."

On the word "love" she falls to the ground and swiftly rolls away, laughing with pleasure and embarrassment.

Technically, this was lovely contact between two partners accustomed to working with each other, and therefore able to take physical risks in a safe and controlled way.

What did we learn? We just saw a rapid physical and verbal exchange with active and playful shifts of dominance. Importantly, there were also moments of stillness that "framed" particularly significant statements (the final moment of flying, while Jason declared his love, for instance). This was a classic session of physicalized banter, with power shifts inherent in the text explicated in the physicality. But because they were honestly responding to each other (nothing forced to fit) there was also some useful information outside of normal text analysis that was revealed in the exchange.

Although Monica is driving the dialogue with her criticism in the first few lines, Jason is controlling the action. He closes his legs to cut off her vision, and then quietly pulls her over while she continues to berate him. Although she seems to be on the attack (always pursuing him, physically as well as verbally), he continues to subversively guide the momentum, most obviously flipping her over with the line "It's not grey," and then taking her on that unexpected flight at the end. In subtle ways as well, he casually entwines his body around hers, taking advantage of the physical leveraging that naturally occurs. This control is not inherent in the text, and is a useful lesson about both characters that we can take away into the rehearsal room. Generally we have learned that they enjoy the banter, and are letting themselves be available to "roll with the punches" as well as deliver them. Although Jason seems passive in this portion of the text, he is always prepared to defend himself—he just does not feel the need unless properly provoked. There was a lot of "testing" of ideas as well as weight and momentum, and a playful acceptance of the curves the other could throw. We see that they really are an equal match.

In a romantic comedy, beats and even tactics and blocking can emerge in the contact. Physicalizing your relationship while arguing allows dominance of weight and motion to mirror the dynamics of the argument—if you had any questions about who was in control in a given moment, look to your physical interaction to clue you in. Sometimes you will be surprised to note that the seemingly receptive character is actually the person driving the action.

Do not try to lock into roles of dominance and submission in the midst of contacting. Allow the roles to shift, and save analysis and observations for afterwards.

Switch partners, and after an initial silent contact, add in text. The same text.

You will find that the same scene is very different with a new partner. Shifts of power will be different, and moments of conflict and resolution may be subtlety altered. This is good. While the text *implies* certain truths about the relationship (as manifested in the dialogue), the real communication is between you two unique individuals playing those roles. There are no absolutes. That is why *Romeo and Juliet* can be played by so many different couples and always be fresh. The basic thrust of the argument underlies their dialogue, but the variations of presentation reflect the personal truth of those two actors.

And there is an extra bonus: working a romantic dialogue through contact improvisation, you stand a greater chance of manifesting "chemistry"—that elusive, visceral attraction between two people. Contact demands the intimacy of complete attention to the other, and purposefully orients the actor to a non-analytical "being" in the moment. You are already engaging in your physical honesty; now paired with an equally honest partner you are well on your way to a compelling chemistry in the scene.

Shakespeare in contact

Shakespearean comedies are fun. The often whimsical or fantastical comedies are full of mistaken identities, cross-purposed lovers, and playful low-lifes. There is almost guaranteed license in Shakespeare's comedies to "play," and the iambic pentameter rhyme scheme is particularly provocative, providing drive, definition, and rhythm for the physical actor. Contacting with any of the comedies promotes an unconscious matching of text and movement complete with punctuation. You do not need to look for rhythmic movement, just allow the character to sincerely speak in a scene and the contact will follow suit. It is not necessary or advisable to find character-appropriate or logical movement: it will only defeat the purpose of free-flowing contact exploration. Physically, as we have noted, one thing leads to another. If you know the scene well, you will be surprised at how effortlessly the physical dialogue and text flow together. In Shakespeare's language, we find hidden jokes and metaphors embedded in the text. Physical metaphors will also emerge if you let them—unconscious manifestations of energy and wit reflecting the content of the lines. These Shakespearean characters are usually bold and clever, and so is their movement.

Not all of these observations apply to every contact improvisation with a Shakespearean scene, but somewhere within the contact improvisation we usually find a dynamic, acrobatic, or combative interaction that matches the energy and spirit of the scene. For instance, in *A Midsummer Night's Dream* the competing ingénues Hermia and Helena might be in a push-me/pull-you movement as they argue, or Helena might be spinning on one leg, as Hermia catches her foot, and both suspend as torrents of accusations emerge. Allow the playfulness of the text in rhythm and content, to inform (but not dictate) the movement. With the playfulness of text supporting the playfulness of physical partnering, Shakespearean comedies are a good way "in" to finding obvious, overt, and sometimes outrageous interaction.

Stand side by side with your scene partner.

Spin around three times, and Freeze!

You have already begun.

(Remember to add text only after establishing a strong contact.)

Now that you have found the physical interaction mirroring speech in a comedy, look to the dramatic plays. Here you will also find that the cleverness of dialogue and punctuation of thought demands reciprocity in movement.

The following is an example from Shakespearean text worked with contact.

Shakespeare's *Hamlet*, Act 3, Scene 4.

Hamlet, Prince of Denmark, confronts his mother the queen after the court has witnessed a performance of Hamlet's "mousetrap play." In the play we see two royal brothers: one murders the other for his crown and marries his queen. In this scene Hamlet attempts to show his mother that the "performance" was a mirror of reality reflecting her recent marriage to his uncle Claudius quickly following the mysterious death of his father.

Hamlet:	Now, mother, what's the matter?
Gertrude:	Hamlet, thou hast thy father much offended.
Hamlet:	Mother, you have my father much offended.
Gertrude:	Come, come, you answer with an idle tongue.
Hamlet:	Go, go, you question with a wicked tongue.
Gertrude:	Why, how now Hamlet!
Hamlet:	What's the matter now?
Gertrude:	Have you forgot me?
Hamlet:	No, by the rood, not so:
	You are the queen, your husband's brother's wife;
	And—would it were not so!—you are my mother.
Gertrude:	Nay, then, I'll set those to you who can speak.
Hamlet:	Come, come and sit you down; you shall not budge:
	You go not till I set you up a glass
	Where you may see the inmost part of you.
Gertrude:	What wilt thou do? Thou wilt not murder me?
	Help, help, ho!

The actors have been contacting both with text and without, and we perceive that there is a cat and mouse game already established; Hamlet is playfully stalking his prey with every move. Gertrude is self-assured but cautious when we begin.

Gertrude sits on the floor, and Hamlet stands with his back to her, slowly twisting back to address her.

"Now mother"

He slowly turns and bends a knee to kneel as she also twists to fully face him. They are both moving in a continuous slow motion.

"What's the matter?"

They are feeling out each other's minimal movements, every subtle shift of weight has a corresponding shift. We see that they are both cautious, on the defensive, and deeply "listening." She places both hands on the floor purposefully and looks up at him saying,

"Hamlet, thou hast thy father much offended."

As she leans in to speak, he unhurriedly shifts his weight back to an upright position of his torso.

"Mother,"

And his knee hits the floor decisively with the word.

"You have my father much offended."

Weight shifts in subtle response, as she hesitantly leans in toward him and then retreats. He mirrors her action, confidently tracking his prey.

"Come, come, you answer with an idle tongue."

The tension between them is palpable, and he speaks quietly.

"Go, go, you question with a wicked tongue."

Suddenly he pounces, and Gertrude rolls out of the way as he lunges and she stands defiantly to face him.

"Why, how now Hamlet!"
"What's the matter now?"

He easily jumps up and moves in on her.

"Have you forgot me?"

She drops to a crouch which he immediately mirrors.

"No"

He bounces back up with the word and feints to the side.

"By the rood, not so:
You are the queen, your husband's brother's wife;"

She jumps back to her feet, and lunges one way and then the other, alert prey ready to sprint, which he counters almost as a defensive sports player blocking her every potential move on cue while continuing,

"And—would it were not so!—you are my mother."

She slaps the floor at the word "mother," and runs by him, saying,

"Nay, then, I'll set those to you that can speak."

He turns his back and pretends to let her run by and then quickly catches up, confronting her.

"Come, come and sit you down; you shall not budge:"

She bends a knee, almost kneeling in a repetition of his previous position, and then suddenly attempts a move sideways. He counters her every hesitant re-positioning with quick attentive counter-moves, continuing,

"You go not till I set you up a glass
Where you may see the inmost part of you."

Her desperate lunges ineffective, she drops back to a crouch on the ground. He kneels and bends toward her, matching her move for move. She speaks,

"What wilt thou do? Thou wilt not murder me?"

She suddenly sprints and he runs spider-like on all fours quickly catching up with her. She is prone now on the ground crying out in her distress.

"Help, help, ho!"

This exchange feels like a sword fight, with feint and parry, retreat and attack. Hamlet is relaxed and relentless in his verbal and physical pursuit. Gertrude is dignified and yet scared, unsure how to proceed in this literal cat and mouse game.

What have we learned that we can take back to the rehearsal hall?

The contact improvisation with text heightened the stakes for both actors in this animalistic pursuit. Survival depended on the next correct statement and the next correct movement. The urgency found in the contact can be infused into a more realistic blocking.

Specifically, the physical punctuation on "Mother" (the knee hits the ground), "you have my father much offended," and the "No" (jump up and sideways feint) "by the rood, not so," is useful. The punctuation is quick and pointed, echoing the rhythm of the text. We also have the series of quick lunges and counter-lunges of "would it were not so!—you are my mother," that again weave the rhythm of text and motion. The implied threat in Hamlet's words has become visibly threatening lunges. This punctuation can easily be transformed to more period appropriate gestures. We now know where.

Dramatic tension was effectively built with the careful, attentive, and dangerous-feeling slow motion opening the scene. Hamlet and Gertrude were almost stalking each other. This stalking is a viable tactic, easy to keep in mind when staging the scene. "You have my father much offended" triggers the first explosion of action followed by another sequence of lines mirrored by intensely slow re-positioning before exploding again in "would it were not so!—you are my mother." Clearly these statements are so important that the characters are driven to reveal their insecurities and passions in violent action. The poker-face can only be maintained as long as no one hits home with truth. Perhaps Gertrude is guilty about marrying her brother in law, and Hamlet's goading taunt "You have my father much offended" makes her roll away. The actions and the pace not only reveal interesting information for the actor (about what lines are important to drive home, and what the tactics might be), but also deliver potential blocking for the director. Your clever body has revealed the essence of the relationship in this scene.

During this contact session, the actor playing Hamlet discovered the playfulness the director had been asking for in the scene (a playfulness of language and action). He toys with Gertrude like a cat with its prey, and mockingly paraphrases her chastisement "Go, go, you question with a wicked tongue" while mirroring her every move. He is both deadly serious and intensely clever, and we need to see both. The *Hamlet* director happened to witness this particular contact session, and realized that he now had a potential tool for guiding the actors in exploratory blocking.

In this context, contact is a viable rehearsal tool, providing vocabulary for the actors, visible energy for the scene, and blocking for the directorial eye.

Ibsen in contact

In all scene work (comedic or dramatic) we find sub-text emerges through contact improvisation. The innermost passions of characters are often revealed through unconscious movement and this is most obvious in contact improvisation with drawing-room text. Chekhov, Ibsen, and Strindberg are all good candidates for scene-work in which the socially appropriate dialogue masks deeper desires.

Stand on the opposite side of the room from your scene partner.

Walk toward each other.

You have already begun.

(Add in text after establishing the movement.)

The following is an example of drawing-room text worked with contact.

Ibsen's *A Doll's House*, Act 1, Scene 6.

This ninteenth-century play is seen as an early feminist statement, supporting a woman's right to financial and intellectual independence. Nora and Torvald are an upper-middle-class married couple; Nora is guilty of overspending and possible forgery, and has just been visited by her secret creditor. Torvald has confronted her with the discovery of this visit, though he does not understand its ramifications.

Torvald: And my little songbird mustn't ever do a thing like that again. No false notes. Isn't that the way it should be? Yes? Of course it is, so let's not talk about it any more. So snug and cozy in here.

Nora: Torvald?

Torvald: Yes?

Nora: I'm terribly excited about the Stenborg's party the day after tomorrow.

Torvald: And I'm terribly curious to see what you'll surprise me with.

Nora: Oh that stupid nonsense!

Torvald: What is?

Nora: It seems so pointless. I can't think of anything to wear.

The actors have been contacting, and the action is quick, responsive, and intent. They do not look at each other. We are not sure if they are playing or struggling. In the midst of rolling and gently colliding, Torvald guides Nora into an unexpected back roll over his prone body. We see now that it is a struggle.

> *"And my little songbird mustn't ever do a thing like that again,"*
> *he says with urgency. "No false notes."*

Nora quickly tries to roll away, stopped by his gentle arm, she twists into an aborted shoulder stand. His arm responding to her action braces her shoulder stand, effectively also pinning her in place.

> *"Isn't that the way it should be?"*

She slowly rolls back down and he sits up in response. She has unwittingly rolled onto his lap. She looks directly at him for the first time, and puts an arm around his neck. Emboldened, he picks up her legs and boldly swivels around into a classic position of protective love, cradling her in his strong arms.

She nods "yes" reluctantly, their heads are almost touching.

"Yes?"

He encourages her, smiling.

The mood has suddenly become complicit and passionate.

Wow. The audience laughs in agreement. This exchange has taken place over the space of ten seconds and two lines, and we are already vicariously eager to experience the next moment in the life of these two characters.

He twists away from her and back around suddenly leaning his weight into her hips, raised now in a low bridge. She is stronger than we think and supports his weight with ease. He enjoys testing her strength, and she watches as he circles around her, always leaning up against her body, until he is fully supported by her strong legs wrapped around his waist. He leans back and mumbles

"Of course it is, so let's not talk about it any more. So snug and cozy in here."

Suddenly the momentum of their mutual weight bowls them over to the side, and he rolls away, grappling one of her legs. There is a pause and they lift heads to look at one another and she suddenly curls submissively around his body, as he once again cradles her. When he cradles her, confining her, she frantically tries to twist away. He kneels in a sturdy tripod position, her leg now hooked over his shoulder, her body draped upside-down, one hand in contact with the floor.

She speaks from this precarious position, once again an unwary victim, her strong body unexpectedly manipulated.

> *"Torvald?"*
> *"Yes?"*
> *"I'm terribly excited about the Stenborg's party the day after tomorrow."*

She extends her leg as she speaks, reaching for the floor without success. He refuses to put her down, although the position also becomes precarious for him, as he struggles to keep balance saying,

> *"And I'm terribly curious to see what you'll surprise me with."*

She arches her body, straining for release, and suddenly twists around, knees bent in a little ball, clinging to his neck saying,

> *"Oh that stupid nonsense!"*
> *"What is?"*

And with the line he loses his balance and they topple to the ground. They relax into the fall, and roll, pausing for a moment head to head to look at each other, and then roll against and away from each other. He stops six feet (two meters) away from her, prone on his stomach, and she lies on her back turning her head to speak to him.

> *"It seems so pointless. I can't think of anything to wear."*

Technically, this was a good contact session. Even in the "conflict" displayed in their exaggerated opposing forces, the two partners have remained intimately sensitive to each other, testing weight, guiding momentum, and cushioning each other in contact with the floor. They were physically safe and relaxed, despite the driving tension of the scene.

What have we learned that we can take back to the rehearsal room?

If we look for generalities, we see Nora repeating movements of clinging dependence and then struggling for release. Torvald is literally pulled off-balance more than once from a dominant position. His unconscious "pinning" of her body in submissive positions fleshes out the metaphor of an oppressive patriarchy quite nicely.

Now what have we learned specifically?

We have learned that Nora reveals unexpected strength (literally supporting Torvald as he mumbles "So let's not talk about it any more").

We have learned that there is a complicit passion and affection between these characters (when they both nod "yes"). This is not explicit in the text, but certainly makes sense, and makes the struggle between them more engaging for the audience—nuanced characters with conflicting desires are much more compelling than linear representations of oppressor and oppressed.

We have learned that a significant beat shift happens as Torvald says "What is?" and then falls over.

We have learned that the moment of agreement (the mutual nod "yes") also initiates a significant beat shift.

The actor playing Nora was surprised to discover that Nora was so deeply conflicted between submission and rebellion (she noted the repeated submissive curling into Torvald's arms juxtaposed to the struggle for release). Both actors agreed that the physical responses contacting the scene were honest, instinctive, and surprising, so she will further explore these conflicting emotions/reactions in her character work. The actor playing Torvald was intrigued to find significant love for Nora expressed in his movement (in addition to the hierarchical superiority he expected from text analysis), and plans to further explore that facet of the character's emotional palette. The information gleaned from contacting a scene is useful in fleshing out the characters, and in finding beats and possible blocking for the scene.

As we observe two fully engaged partners contacting with an Ibsen scene, we see physical as well as verbal moments of conflict and resolution, the sub-text is literally played out. Who is driving the scene, who has the power at a given moment is literally depicted— we see overt manifestations of hidden desires. Note moments of extreme physical shifts; as we have seen in the *Doll's House* scene, they often correlate to emotional shifts of the characters.

Your scene has been actively worked in contact several times

You and your partner have shared perceptions about sub-text and rhythmic shifts of power in the scene as revealed through the contact.

Stop.

This time you are going to contact (still allowing the intrinsic emotional/physical connection to emerge), but using only period appropriate movements.

We re-visit *A Doll's House.*

Torvald stands behind Nora, and placing a hand on her shoulder, moves in slightly closer saying urgently,

> *"And my little songbird mustn't ever do a thing like that again."*

Nora curls her shoulder in at his touch, and as his hand drops she turns around toward him leading with her shoulder. His head tilts in expectation of an apology. She fluctuates and, avoiding eye contact, she gracefully swivels back the way she came and walks tentatively away. He resolutely steps forward in pursuit, and she suddenly turns back to him unintentionally moving into his extended arm, which now drapes around her shoulder, effectively pinning her in place.

> *"Isn't that the way it should be?"*

She continues to avoid his gaze, and reaches for the armchair that is behind him, and before she can reach it, he sits and unexpectedly pulls her into his lap. She curls her arm around his neck, and he lowers his head to hers asking,

> *"Yes?"*

She nods shyly in agreement and they both smile, complicit in the moment.

What has happened here? The blocking has taken on the energy and intention of the full-out contact, but is now subtler, and more based in drawing-room realism. Twisting rolls on the floor that gently collide and ricochet away have become the hesitant dance of drawing-room decorum: a hand on the shoulder initiates a response of the shoulder turning in slightly and then twisting ever so slightly away, taking the body with it in a few graceful steps. The surprise moment remains when Torvald takes control and wins agreement in the mutual nod "yes." The surprise blocking of Torvald pulling Nora onto his lap has even found its way into the drawing-room.

Physical movements become smaller and more subtle as you transfer your improv to the drawing-room. But the rhythms and intentions remain the same. Attentive physical alertness to the other has not diminished—it has instead transformed to subtle and discreet interaction. The ever-important energy exchange, conveyed in everyday gestures and manners, holds a whole new power. The audience is engaged, again, by the relationship between you. A slow release of the chest and inclination of the head can trigger a response in your partner (a sudden stiffening of their back) that draws the audience. They are viscerally engaged with the physical truth of your relationship.

Connected to the rhythm and content of the language and connected to your partner, your physicality is aligned with your character's world and intentions.

If you have the opportunity, watch another pair contact with a drawing-room scene, and witness their progression from extreme full-out contact to realism-based contact. Usually as the physical impulses are transferred to realistic movement, the character mask comes into play. This "masking" of true impulse is a natural human response in most social situations and is what keeps us from bluntly enacting our deepest desires at all times. Overt sub-text, even in realistic gestures, is not always what is called for on the theatrical stage.

Improvise through the scene a second time with realistic motion, and let the improv play itself out; often the honest physicality is naturally tempered by the character sometimes revealing and sometimes masking sub-text. If you find that your contact does not naturally incorporate masking, you can at this point make some conscious choices about when to allow impulse to be revealed. But it is rare that the driving force of a good contact does not naturally bring many levels of physical/emotional and social response into play.

Contemporary drama in contact

We return to contemporary theater—in this case, drama.

Good contemporary drama has a visceral realism in language and action that reflects our expanded attitudes about what is portrayable on stage and screen. The "inferred" sexual encounter of a 1940s Tenessee Williams play might be graphically described in a 1990s David Mamet script. Many writers of stage and screen overtly explore intimacy and violence in settings of chilling familiarity from impoverished back-roads in Texas, to the apparent gloss of a corporate boardroom. And it should be familiar—they are holding up the mirror to us NOW. Actors work such scripts to flex their muscles of embodiment—there is no distance. These are the characters of today, speaking in the language of today without a filter of stylization or romanticism.

AUTHENTICITY

I sat in a darkened theater in Rouen, France several years ago—an invited panelist for a discussion about the "U.S. Theatre Invisible." The theater was hot, outside it was raining and it was the end of a long day of panel discussions finalized over a congenial meal with excellent wine. I was relaxing my hold on the French language when a torrent of words came from the stage. A young woman sat next to me, avidly watching this workshop production of Naomi Wallace's *In the Heart of America*, a work known for its street-wise dialogue. The production was in French, the scene was about two GIs daring each other in war games and was spoken in a rapid-fire ping-pong match of language. The woman next to me listened in absolute attentive silence, along with the rest of the packed house. When the lights came up after appreciative applause, and someone congratulated her shyly in English, I realized that I was sitting next to the playwright. After my own congratulations, I asked "What did you think about the interpretation?" Naomi Wallace's work, after all, is known for its colloquial authenticity—it seemed un-translatable. Without hesitation she said, "I don't understand French, but I liked it a lot." "Why?" "It wasn't sentimental."

Authenticity is perceived some place beyond language.

Sam Shepard, David Mamet, and Naomi Wallace scripts (among others) are all good candidates for material that is rich in colloquial language and imagery. Stakes are high in these scenes, and such no-holds barred honesty requires an equal authenticity in portrayal.

Stand facing your partner and touch fingertips.

Take one step back away from each other (you will be compelled to lean against each other's hands).

Take another step back away from each other (keep leaning).

Take a third step back away (keep leaning).

You have already begun!

The following is an example of a contemporary drama worked with contact.

JP Miller's *The Days of Wine and Roses,* excerpts from the final scene of the 1962 television drama about alcoholism.

Joe and Kirsten are an en-stranged married couple who are both dealing with addiction. Joe has been sober for a year, and tries to convince his struggling wife to join him in recovery.

Joe: I want to love you Kirs, but I'm afraid of you. I'm an alcoholic. I can't take a drink. But I'm afraid of what we do to each other. If only you'd say you'd try . . .

Kirsten: You're strong Joe. That's why I know you can help me. If only we had it back like it was—

Joe: Back like it was—! Do you remember how it really was Kirs? It was you and me and booze. A threesome. A threesome! . . . I am not going to drink with you.

Kirsten: I wouldn't ask you to drink with me. I'd control myself.

Joe: You can't control yourself! You're an alcoholic, same as I am.

Kirsten: No!

Joe: You and I were a couple of drunks on a sea of booze in a leaky boat! And it sank! But I've got hold of something to keep me from going under, and I'm not going to let it go, not for you, not for anybody. If you want to grab on, grab on, but there's only room for you and me. No threesome.

The two actors in this scene have been contacting with this text earlier in the session. The mood is intimate, vulnerable, and dangerous. The actor playing Joe is kneeling, and the actress playing Kirsten stands at his back bending over to wrap her arms around his chest. They both face out, his face averted as he speaks

"I want to love you Kirs,"

He suddenly stretches his arm upwards, passionately touching her unseen face.

"But I'm afraid of you."

With a sudden burst of energy he pushes her away, using the momentum to twist away from her, and she complies limply spinning to sit on the ground not looking at him.

"I'm an alcoholic."

He lunges toward her and in perfect causality she backswings a limp arm toward him and he rolls as if hit, thumping onto the floor on his back.

"I can't take a drink. But I'm afraid of what we do to each other."

She limply rolls toward him and they are still for a moment, then sense each other tentatively, responding in small shifts of weight, crawling on their hands and knees.

"If only you'd say you'd try . . ."
She murmurs,
"You're strong Joe. That's why I know you can help me."

In response, he rolls and fluidly reaches his arms around her waist and hides his face in her hair and rocks her. She holds his arms in place now around her shoulders, and says wistfully,

"If only we had it back like it was—"

He pulls her in tighter to himself, then pauses and violently pushes her body away, projecting himself with the momentum into a circle around her, pushing her away by her head and then feigning lunges. She dodges and spins away from his attacks and, in final desperation to connect, leaps into his arms as he circles around her. Stunned for an instant, he carries her weight, arms grappling his neck, legs entwined around his waist, and then purposefully lowers her to the ground. He gives one final push of her head before he follows the momentum to an exhausted roll onto the floor. As he rolls within her range she grasps one of his legs and he wearily begins,

"Back like it was—! Do you remember how it really was Kirs?"

He rolls away, puts hands on the ground and as he pushes himself up to standing is caught mid-action with a foot in the air, as she nestles her neck against his upraised foot. He cannot stand, but continues to speak quietly, intently.

"It was you and me and booze. A threesome. A threesome!"

And as he continues to talk, he brings both feet up, carefully balancing on his hands and slowly moving his weight onto her neck and upper back. She twists to a sturdier position trapped as he kneels on her upper back. Then he slowly slides down her crouching body encircling her with his arms, hands clutching her hair. They both breathe in this silent moment, and he says quietly,

"I am not going to drink with you."

He rolls onto his back pulling her over on top of him and they roll apart and she immediately ricochets back to him saying,

"I wouldn't ask you to drink with me."

She crawls toward him to tell him a secret.

"I'd control myself."

He crouches in complete stillness as she nuzzles his shoulder with her head, and without looking at her he says,

"You can't control yourself! You're an alcoholic, same as I am."

She violently pushes now against his shoulder, and they push shoulder to shoulder against each other to stand as she cries,

"No!"

She spins away and lifts an arm to strike, and he turns to her and lifts her suddenly, paces the room carrying her clinging over his shoulder, and with controlled violence and a sudden bang, sets her down, and walks away. When she follows, he methodically and quickly rolls her to the ground and straddles her, hands at her neck—they breathe and look each other directly in the eyes. And she suddenly reverses the move, straddling his body, holding his hands in her own as he speaks.

"You and I were a couple of drunks on a sea of booze in a leaky boat! And it sank!"

He rolls to his side and she is carried by the momentum.

"But I've got hold of something to keep me from going under, and I'm not going to let it go,"

With sudden energy he topples her over, stands, and pulls her up to kneeling facing him, supporting her head in his hands and looking directly into her eyes.

"Not for you, not for anybody."

He suddenly twists and she is in his arms in a violent embrace—they kiss and she holds him tight as he whispers,

"If you want to grab on, grab on, but there's only room for you and me. No threesome."

This was a riveting contact—vulnerable, fluid, and appropriately violent. It was so intimate that it felt voyeuristic for the observers.

This is a scene about desperate need, both to hold on to each other and for Joe to hold on to the sobriety he has attained. The "needs" are palpable in this contact, as is Joe's refusal, literally "pushing away" Kirsten. The actors were so physically connected to these needs and to each other that there was never a feeling of language or emotion being "pushed." Observers afterwards remarked that it was as if these were the *only* words that could be spoken.

Actors dropped lines, but interestingly, they also repeated phrases during significant beat changes, as if the character were letting the thought sink in deeper. Both actors allowed themselves to be changed by the other, movement was completely fluid, relaxed, and synchronistic despite the high drama of the scene. Also interestingly, most text was spoken with head averted: the actors were either avoiding eye contact or literally so closely bound to each other that they could not "see." The moments of direct eye contact were notable and held, so that they became moments of importance. Physical metaphors for "co-dependence," "stifling" and the barely averted "strangling" were liberating for the actors to instinctively embody. The actor playing Joe commented that he had not thought of the scene as being so violent, but he affirmed that the contact session felt emotionally correct. This excerpt of text taken out of context could have been melodramatic. Instead, the physical and emotional commitment of the actors and their fearlessness to really listen and respond underlined the poignancy of the situation.

What can we take back to the rehearsal room beyond the observations about beats and repeated phrases, the powerful moments of eye contact, and the mutual clinging gestures? There was a bonus lesson that became apparent working through this scene:

Do not be afraid to play the positive objective.

It is a given in actor training that one cannot play a negative—actors are encouraged to find an objective or goal for their character, so that even the most depressed or evil character cannot play "depressed" or "evil." The character must strive for something (something perhaps that they do not obtain, perhaps something erroneous). Contact improvisation by its very nature demands that both participants be actively engaged in an energy and weight exchange. Scenes explored through contact have active physical/emotional commitment from both actors. In this case, the actress playing Kirsten found her character far more sympathetic than she had previously seen her. She had previously seen Joe as being victimized by Kirsten. Now she felt that they were both victims. After this contact session she commented that now she wanted to re-write the script. This is a wonderful actor's response. She does not need to re-write the script, she needs to positively play the passion and objectives that were uncovered through the physical work. The through-line of the script will take care of itself, or the director will shape it. The newly emphasized positive action, her yearning for connection with Joe, turns *The Days of Wine and Roses* exchange into a desperate dialogue between two equally vulnerable human beings, and that exchange becomes powerful theater.

How much of the literal physical action that happened during this studio session can we take back to the more conventional stage? Contact improvisation with such highly dramatic material can translate into a literal template for blocking, as we will see with the next scene.

Patrick Marber's *Closer*, Act 1, Scene 6.

***Closer* is a contemporary British drama about two couples in London and their various sexual and psychological re-groupings. The actors were particularly interested in working this scene because of the explicit revelations and high stakes (a married couple confess their mutual infidelity). *Closer* is a play where duplicitous sexual activity is masked by proper manners and cool exteriors, so how then to honestly play this brutal confrontation?**

Larry:	Anna . . . You're leaving me because you think you don't deserve happiness, but you do Anna, you do . . . Did you have a bath because you had sex with him? So you didn't smell of him? So you'd feel less *guilty*?
	And how do you *feel*?
Anna:	Guilty.
Larry:	Did you ever love me?
Anna:	*Yes*.
Larry:	Big fucking deal.
	Anna . . . please, don't leave me . . .*please*.
	Did you do it here?
Anna:	No.
Larry:	Why not? Just tell me the truth.
Anna:	Yes, we did it here.
Larry:	Where?
Anna:	Here.
Larry:	On this? (*He gestures to the chaise longue*)
	We had our first fuck on this.
	Think of *me*?
	When?
	When did you do it here?
	ANSWER THE FUCKING QUESTION.
Anna:	This evening.
Larry:	Did you come?
Anna:	Why are you doing this?

Larry: Because I want to know.
Anna: Yes . . . I came.
Larry: How may times?
Anna: Twice.
Larry: How?
Anna: First he went down on me and then we fucked.
Larry: Who was where?
Anna: I was on top and then he *fucked me from behind.*
Larry: And that's when you came the second time?
Anna: *Why is the sex so important?*
Larry: BECAUSE I'M A FUCKING CAVEMAN.

The actors have been working this scene with contact and text. We find them now in the middle of Larry's stunned response having discovered that Anna has been unfaithful throughout their marriage. The mood is explosive, unsure, and hyper-attentive.

The actor playing Anna rolls away from her partner, and he chases her, until she twists to a cross-legged sit, cringing away from him. He reaches for her and her forward momentum reverses rocking her weight back against his body. She unravels to the floor, and there is a brief pause as his hand protects her head from hitting the ground just in time. They look at each other.

> *"Anna . . . You're leaving me because you think you don't deserve happiness,"*

He slowly turns sideways, his bent leg effectively framing her stiffened torso, slowly rolling her over,

> *"but you do Anna, you do . . ."*

He finishes the controlling movement inadvertently rolling himself face first against the ground, and she uses the opportunity to quietly twist away from him. He rocks up to sitting and she does the same in response a foot away from him, hyper-alert. He speaks to her back,

> *"Did you have a bath"*

She slowly leans her back toward him as he speaks and he responds recoiling,

"*because you had sex with him?*"

She gently turns to face him and reaches out.

"*So you didn't smell of him? So you'd feel less guilty?*"

Kneeling, she moves toward him and he leans back, propped up on his hands facing her, long legs extended. She tentatively touches one of his feet and he instantly recoils.

"*And how do you feel?*"

She crouches, avoiding his gaze.

"*Guilty.*"

He slowly stands, tentative, caught between reaching for her and backing away.

"*Did you ever love me?*"

She reaches for him.

"*Yes.*"

And runs to catch up with him—he has already started pacing away from her, spitting out,

"*Big fucking deal.*"

She catches up with him and leaps onto his back—he staggers with her unexpected weight and pauses, again seemingly caught between throwing her off and accepting her embrace.

"*Anna . . . please, don't leave me . . . please.*"

While he speaks, she quietly lowers herself to the ground, and he recovers his balance from the release of her weight. There is a small pause, and he says,

"*Did you do it here?*"

She rocks to a kneeling position facing away from him.

"No."

He quickly spins to face her.

"Why not?"

He slides into her, grabs her side, and puts his face in her neck.

"Just tell me the truth."

She wriggles her shoulders in discomfort and averts her head twisting away from him.

"Yes, we did it here."
"Where?"
"Here."

She twists upstage now, but not out of his grasp.

He almost seductively says,

"On this?" (pointing at the imaginary chaise longue)

He manipulates her struggling body to the ground and straddles her.

"We had our first fuck on this. Think of me? When? When did you do it here?"

He struggles to stand and picks up both of her legs now as she squirms to get away.

"ANSWER THE FUCKING QUESTION."

He forces both of her feet toward her torso, straddling her, and effectively pinning her awkwardly against the ground.

"This evening"
"Did you come?"

She struggles to get away and he pins her body with one leg as she cries,

"Why are you doing this?"
"Because I want to know."
"Yes . . . I came."

He finally releases his hold, and she pushes him off, and rolls away. He pursues.

"How many times?"
"Twice."
"How?"

Quickly crawling he catches up with her, and pulls her back toward himself, making her look at him.

"First he went down on me and then we fucked."
"Who was where?"

He grabs her hips and as she struggles angrily to twist out of his grip, he crawls onto her back, covering her body with his,

"I was on top, and then he fucked me from behind.*"*
"And that's when you came the second time?"

He re-positions himself on top of her and she angrily twists onto her back.

"Why is the sex so important?"

He turns her over onto her stomach again, and pins her with the length of his body yelling,

"BECAUSE I'M A FUCKING CAVEMAN."

This is so literal as to be almost pornographic—the rhythm of argument, the dialogue and movement were all powerfully intertwined. The struggle for sexual dominance in this no-holds-barred fight barely kept within the realm of "civilized behavior."

So is this legitimate blocking for the scene?

For all practical purposes, yes! The play is about deception and unexpected reversals and reveals. The overtly sexual displays of dominance after the tentativeness of Larry's original questioning felt boldly authentic as staging. The actors were emotionally and physically engaged, the observers were surprised and appropriately provoked. Action and words both existed in the same realistic realm (this scene is about a married couple in the privacy of their apartment after all—anything can happen). If the scene was envisioned as a slightly heightened "reality" within the context of the play, the sex and violence of the dialogue had perfect portrayal in the movement.

But in this particular production, the director envisioned a continuation of the mask, and wanted to keep the hurt and anger and psychological manipulation under civilized wraps. So is the contact session still valid? Absolutely. The actors felt they had hit new strides by running the scene in contact improvisation. Both felt more honestly connected to this difficult material and, particularly for the actor playing Larry, the experience of allowing the hurt and violence to emerge physically was liberating. Larry's progression from hurt and confusion to retaliation and control was explicit in the movement. The physical memory of this visceral contact can clearly inform the acting, and can even inform a more restrained staging. In fact, the physical tension of repression has its own dramatic power. Larry must now teeter on the edge of self-control with sudden bursts of release (perhaps even using some of the extreme movements found in the contact) indicating the turmoil beneath. The actors have this experience in their bodies now, and it is useful as a muscle memory of desire and dominance.

What general lessons can we take back to the rehearsal room from these two scenes?

The relationship between the two characters in a scene is already present, even before anyone begins talking. Text is the secondary realization of that relationship. Physicality comes even before language.

Physical extremes and physical metaphors are useful to enact. In a realistic staging, Joe will not crouch on Kirsten's shoulders, "crushing" her attempts to cling, but the metaphor is useful to enact. Allow your intelligent body to express, and then look at that expression afterwards. *Let your body give you information.* You many learn something new about the character.

Violence—passion in romance, passion in hate. Let it out with sound. Joe wanted to slam Kirsten into the ground, but instead the actor used his good contacting instincts to lower his partner to the ground, slamming his foot in punctuation. There were two instances of violent slamming in *The Days of Wine and Roses* in which the contactors took excellent care of each other and allowed sound to express the violence of intent.

The rhythm of the exchange can translate to the stage using more "realistic" movement, but using the same rhythm as the contact session. For instance, the rhythmic pauses in Joe's lines, "I want to love you Kirs, but I'm afraid of you. I'm an alcoholic. I can't take a drink. But I'm afraid of what we do to each other," were full of intention. He physically went from reaching for her, to pushing her away, to pursuing her as she fell and then being knocked over by her weak response. And then they both tentatively "tested" each other out. He can have those same intentions and responses in context appropriate movement, and the text can be interspersed at the same revealing rhythm within the blocking.

Summary: fabulous information about character was gained in both of these scenes. The actor playing Kirsten discovered the victimization of her character, the actors playing Larry and Anna were allowed to feel and enact the nuances of betrayal, guilt, and retaliation. We saw the inevitable heightened awareness and engagement with the other that contact demands. Blocking using contact improvisation can be visceral, literal, and shockingly appropriate for the contemporary drama. And if aesthetic choices lead elsewhere, you can let the rhythmic relationship between text and movement inform. Fundamentally, allow the re-enforced connection between partners to inform the blocking.

For the courageous physical actor using contact improvisation as the way into a dramatic scene, the physical relationship between two characters is the primary reality, and the ensuing dialogue is the secondary expression of that reality.

We have come full circle, from the movement studio back to the stage, addressing an actor's needs through physical training. The articulated body, receptive to impulse and responsive to the partner, actively engages in the task at hand with the necessary tools.

You have already begun.

CHAPTER 6

Active Imagination: Performance Composition

By using the tools of the previous chapters, you are physically and perceptively prepared for the stage. But alongside a disciplined and alert body, the physical actor has a final responsibility—to bring into play the active imagination.

Creation and communication are the reasons we are drawn to theater, and the inventiveness of childhood "pretend" (whether it be candy-land journeys or adventures in untamed jungles) is critical to the development of the well-rounded person. By inventing we learn to allow possibility, and learn to live vicariously through imaginary situations and imaginary people. So too, imagination and the act of creating personal work develops an important aspect of the strong physical actor. Much like the child, you explore worlds only you can imagine, and in expressing those worlds you come back full circle to the actor's initial reason for existence—communication. Presenting your own original movement/theater work, you communicate something so real, so personal, and so vividly imagined that it enlarges the audience's experience, and allows them to vicariously live that world through you. Three things are needed for physical creation: the first is to unlock the active imagination, the second is to employ communicative tools (in this case movement vocabulary and an articulated body), and the third is to structure your images in such a way that the audience can go with you. Although you may not hold aspirations to become a choreographer or playwright, the physical actor gains creative confidence and a certain mental prowess through the act of creating, of daring to imagine and then actively framing and presenting what has been imagined. It is as important to exercise your creative muscle as it is to have mastery over any physical technique in this book. The physically disciplined actor without an active imagination is a one-dimensional being, useful, but limited in range. But the creative physical actor becomes a conduit for the active imagination, and presentational structure allows creativity to have shape and muscle.

The following simple exercises encourage the development of creativity. We further explore "instant art" (mentioned in Chapter 2, Space) and fundamental exercises for physical theater creation. In this chapter we will also explore how to structure the active imagination into very personal movement pieces. These exercises and concepts are meant to be explored at the same time as the technical work in Chapters 3 (Mime) and 4 and 5 (Partnering and Contact Improvisation). Included are guidelines for group composition: how to find abstract vocabulary, and how to position and move groups in space for optimum dramatic impact. Flexing creative muscle while learning technique is a great way to process information, to personalize it, and to make it your own.

"Instant art"

Fast and extreme improvisations are "instant art." There is no time to mentally construct; the only option is to connect to the given image, situation, or emotion, and MOVE. "Instant art" demands immediate response and the results with physically trained and fearless actors appear almost choreographed with complicity of motion and engaging stage picture. Honed instincts, good partnering listening, and an ability to follow a dictated beat are the obvious skills practiced, but in the context of developing creativity, we appreciate these exercises for their imaginative connection. They are a means of going from guided imagery to creative action. The following are three exercises explored earlier in the book, but this time presented as useful tools for movement creation.

1 *Amoeba (Chapter 2, Space)* This exercise based on complicit group motion is beneficial for developing group responsiveness while maintaining integrity of individual action. It can also be used as a choreographic exercise when specific imagery is attached to the motion. You will find that the images used will trigger highly dramatic physicalization.

2 *Freeze frames (Chapter 2, Space)* The immediate response to count and imagine is frozen in space for us to view. Freeze frames encourage instantly expressive physicality, and can be practiced solo or with a partner. The imagery created is in response to a dictated situation. These are frozen sequential moments in time.

3 *Statuary (Chapter 3, Mime)* Imagery again connects to physicality, but this time you are molded by a partner, the resulting statue a three-dimensional, immobile representation of an emotion. This exercise provides easy access to creative impulse, and it also gives fabulously detailed physical/emotional moments.

After experiencing the complicit nature and immediate gratification of "instant art," you are now ready for your first planned group creation.

Circus act

You are working with a group of at least four other actors. Your goal is to create a circus, complete with ringmaster, name, and lots of impossible circus acts. You have ten minutes. Go.

The ten minutes usually turns into fifteen or twenty minutes as creative actors given time to actually plan, become enamored with their scenarios. This is a low pressure, highly creative improv situation—no one is a trained circus performer with equipment on hand, so everyone needs to invent impossible tasks of courage and skill. Or at least, present the task as if it were impossible. "Circus" gives automatic license for creative play: wild animals, acrobats, clowns, and tightrope walkers will appear alongside the proverbial strongman and Siamese twins. Mimetic ropes and balls, as well as concepts of causality, immobility, and counterbalance are at your disposal. With such riches, a performing group quickly begins to understand the value of directed presentation. If everyone performs a separate act at once, the audience sees a jumble of action. So the actors also gain a director's eye—focusing the audience's attention on the tightrope walker (perhaps by drumming an accelerating beat on the ground to accompany her accelerating tricks), and then shifting into the next performer's act of derring-do. Actors learn how to make the most of presentational bravado, and an "acrobat" boldly venturing to stand on one leg (!) can get a wildly enthusiastic audience response. It all depends on how the tension was built and how the resulting climactic achievement is framed by the other performers.

Clown funeral

Work with at least four other actors. You have ten minutes.

Go.

The situation is rife with comic potential. Clowns are vulnerable. Clowns are sincere. Clowns sincerely "try" and inevitably fail. And that is why they are so funny. They are just like us. Fearless creativity is demanded as these creatures, full of personal integrity, perform this sad ritual. But because they are clowns, of course, anything can go wrong.

The clown funeral is one of my favorite creative exercises. It demands a similar investment as the circus, but a more low-key performance energy (it is, after all, a funeral). In presenting the clown funeral, compositional structure and framing are critical, as the sympathetic audience follows the developing conflict and resolution.

After each exercise discuss perceptions and observations. The audience will be able to give feedback on whether actions were clearly delineated and if they could follow the sequence of events.

Movement theater creation

First, find out what it is you have to say. To create original work in any field you need to be invested in the communication, and you need to "own" the topic. While in the process of developing work, searching for vocabulary or sequence, you can always return with confidence to your essential message, what it is that you have to say. Original work takes a commitment of time, energy, and thought. Clarification of your ideas is crucial to physical expression—so do not choose lightly. Let ideas percolate in the bathtub or when walking the dog. Talk with your colleagues about subjects that compel you. Read literature, go to museums, and allow yourself to dream around an idea. Once a subject has emerged, you are ready to begin the creative process of structuring and developing movement theater.

CREATIVE HONESTY

Barney Simon, a South African theater artist noted for creating and directing brave new theater work based on group process, was commissioned to work with a group of young actors in the United States. Their objective was to create a collective work under Barney's guidance. The actors were honored and excited to work with this master, and Barney, in late night sessions with cigarettes and coffee, explained his creative process. Accustomed to working in a country fraught with political strife and social and economic inequities, the subject of his theater was inevitably linked to the burning injustice in his performer's lives. Subjects were personal and vital: milk denied mothers by federal agencies, curfew and related killings in apartheid-ruled South Africa. As Barney sat with his talented and eager American actors searching for the subject of their communal creation, it became clear that finding commonality was difficult. Actors brought up topics relevant to contemporary life—aids, poverty, and drugs—and each suggestion was discarded. "Do you have aids?" Barney asked. "Is dealing with this a part of your daily life? If not, we need to find another subject; we need to find what IS critical to you. If the most important thing in your life is going to the mall on the weekends, THAT is what this project should be about."

Individual honesty is the beginning. Ultimately this project became a series of personal vignettes reflecting the disparate lives of the actors. As an individual creator, your task is simplified, but the same deep honesty is demanded.

Movement theater: the rules

These are rules that are helpful with early work.

1   *Projects should be between one and seven minutes long, and absolutely no longer*   Error is usually made on the side of being too long as opposed to being too short. Once the creative juices begin flowing the novice wants to put in everything they have discovered and the kitchen sink. Edit yourself. Say one thing clearly.

2   *Have a clear beginning, middle, and end*   Even the most abstract work needs to have a starting point, trajectory, climax, and resolution.

3   *Begin and end with a freeze*   You will be amazed at how often the studio audience, without benefit of stage lighting, is not sure when a movement piece actually began or ended.

4   *Give us a title before you begin*   This little hint is often helpful, giving us a context by which to view your work.

The guidelines

Given these absolute rules, the following guidelines will aid in the creative process.

Props: can be used, as can costumes; however, make sure that whatever you use is necessary to your movement piece. The single chair that becomes a vehicle when turned upside down and an obstacle when turned with its back to the audience is expressively necessary, as opposed to an entire set of living room furniture placed on stage just to create ambience.

Costumes: can evoke strong images, and simple costume pieces, such as a scarf, can help character transformation, but should also be used judiciously, and never just for decorative purposes.

Music: can guide a movement theater piece but, as mentioned earlier, as theater artists our primary allegiance is to the dramatic relationship. While structuring elements of dance in shape, motion, and rhythm are also structuring elements of physical theater, we need to use music to help convey our message, and not allow the music to use us. So do not act out the lyrics to a song.

This is the final, but perhaps most important guideline:

Use movement theater for what it does best: silent stage action mouthing words shows us that words are called for here, and that movement theater is not the correct medium. The physical techniques of mime, and the vocabulary found in contact improvisation partnering are all potential means of expression. Movement theater is a physical communication that presents theatrical imagery through the expressive body in space. Time, place, and even character can transform. Or not. But as a theatrical event, we are deeply interested in conveying our statement—whether it is a complex sequence of movements for six performers, or the simple articulated unfolding of a body, there is a final meaning to the action.

The ways and means: techniques and devices

Technique

As mentioned, you already have a physical vocabulary for movement theater—mime isolations and illusions, partnering lifts and rolls, and simple walking are all potentially choreographed motion. Physical shapes found in warm-up exercises, freeze frames, amoeba, trading fours, or statuary are other sources of vocabulary. Mine any other dance techniques, martial arts forms or even sports vocabulary that you already have. What you do with the technique is what is important.

Devices

Speed

Slow motion is beautiful to look at. We enjoy the shifting of balance, the counterbalanced extensions and the shapes created by the slowly moving body. Slow motion makes a strong statement juxtaposed to normal motion, and gives the audience time to consider the slow motion action. All of these are reasons why slow motion is used so often in film to show the impact of the bullet or the meeting of two lovers, and it can be used with equal power on the stage.

Immobility

A moment frozen in time; the sculpture of a body expressing deep emotion. These are powerful means of making a statement within movement theater.

Physical rhythms

As discussed earlier in the contact improvisation scene work, rhythms naturally change in any good conversation. If everything has the same emphasis, nothing is more important than everything else. Physical rhythmic changes are equally important in creating movement pieces. There is a rhythmic framing of moments, a build leads to a climax and denouement in literature, music, and theater. The same is true in movement theater. Accelerating emotion or discovery has corresponding physical rhythm.

Causality

An action demands reaction, and whether it is a ball tossed from one hand and caught by the other, or a wave of motion that is initiated by one lone performer and received simultaneously by three others, causality is an effective demonstration of relationship.

Borrowing: creation with training wheels

Borrowing: poetry

Striking art works can inspire artists in other fields. Great classical composers create music based on literature or painting (Grieg's "Peer Gynt," or Mussorgsky's "Pictures at an Exhibition"), and poetry can be inspired by mythology (Rilke's "Orpheus" series).

Choose a poem and create a movement theater work based on this poem. You may have it read aloud while you perform, you may perform in silence and show the poem afterwards, or you may create your work based on the theme of the poetry, and never share the poem itself. You decide.

This is creation with training wheels because you have the option to let the structure of the poem be the structure of your movement piece, dictating content and rhythm. However, it is still your responsibility to make the text physically manifest, literally fleshing out the imagery of the poem.

Borrowing: visual art

Find a painting, piece of sculpture, or art photograph that engages you deeply. This is the starting point of your movement theater creation.

Visual art encompasses both imagery (a young girl, a vase, or three intersecting lines) *and* rhythm, shape, and color. A movement piece inspired by a John Singer Sargeant portrait might reflect the life of the model; while a project inspired by three intersecting lines might be a study of geometric trajectories of three performers moving through space. Or the round blue vase with explosively brilliant red flowers painted by Matisse might become an abstraction of rotund shape topped by explosive motion that resolves itself literally in a depiction of the artist at an easel painting in small minimal brushstrokes. Do not be afraid to combine literal and abstract images in the same piece. Your intelligent audience likes the challenge of connecting internal and external worlds. Just be clear about what it is you want to say. One of the unique properties of movement theater as an art form is the ability to transform. Time and place can change, and one performer can play many characters in the space of a short movement theater work. The transformative property of physical theater gives license to the creative artist to create an entire world and sequence of events that the audience accepts as logical. You create the rules, just be clear about what you want to say and remain consistent with the conventions that you use to say it.

Borrowing: other forms

Create original work based on:

- Obituaries
- Maps
- Old postcards (text and/or image).

Movement theater: construction

Once you have an idea about what topic you want to address—for instance, you want to create a piece about your father—you need to clarify "what" about your father is compelling. Is it his eccentric habit of wearing bow ties, or his glorious career as a saxophone player in amateur bands, or his inability to cook anything except spaghetti? Let's say that you want to focus on his cooking skills. Your father is a methodical man and must carefully organize his ingredients before cooking. So now we know that there must be a performer carefully arranging objects in space.

At this point begin to experiment with arranging objects.

Following are two different scenarios of movement theater creation based on the same premise. These are here as examples of the many, many different approaches that can be taken in construction of a movement theater project.

Scenario 1

You are arranging the cooking ingredients. You will find that your actions become exaggerated. Mimetic accuracy is accompanied by little sound effects (the can opener, the squeaky cupboard door).

The audience revels in the bravura performance of repeated precise actions and sounds, and the cook's quiet satisfaction in the orderly kitchen.

Now the cooking project becomes a little clown show as the methodical organization backfires, and like the sorcerer's apprentice, the well-laid imaginary space (full of ingredients) transforms in an uncontrollable escalation of activity (the water boils over, and you burn yourself, reaching for a towel you spill cheese everywhere).

Frantic (but accurate) activity gets faster and faster making the situation worse, and at the apex of frustration you move into a slow-motion scream, kicking invisible dishes and finally beating the spaghetti pot to death in your silent slow-motion aria.

Silence.

You lift your head and survey the destroyed kitchen, the rational organized person viewing the perplexing landscape of cooking as a voice from off-stage calls "Honey, is dinner ready yet?"

Scenario 2

One by one three performers enter the stage and become your "objects."

As you stir sauce in a bowl, they join right hands and spin in a circle. As they are "stirred," your stirring motions transfer to your chest.

The trio behind you breaks into a duet jitterbugging, alternating the third person outside the action. The trio is happy in the exchange and shifts of partner are effortlessly playful.

Meanwhile you are affected by the flirtateous activity, and the stirring motions travel to your hips, and then to your knees, until you too step into the partnering.

We now have two couples jitterbugging. You effortlessly switch partners and weight and energy exchange adjusts to this new person.

You switch one final time, now to the most unlikely partner.

The four of you dance as a group, breaking into joyous unison, each performer initiating a step that the others repeat culminating in a celebratory combination of all the steps.

One by one the performers drop out of the dance and take their place on stage as "objects" leaving only you, the oblivious cook dancing with abandon.

Then the voice comes from off-stage, "Honey, is dinner ready yet?"

Discussion

We have two different movement pieces, each based on the same premise, the difficulties of cooking spaghetti. In the first scenario our solo performer uses mime technique with sound effects, rhythmic escalation, and slow motion to convey his frustration with cooking. In the second movement piece, isolations and partnering techniques are used along with some simple choreographic sequencing to convey the cook's pleasant daydream.

In neither of these scenarios do we understand that this is a movement piece about your father, and perhaps that is not important. This is not charades after all—you are creating art and it comes from some place very personal and real for you. Whether the audience understands your source is immaterial. The universality of day-dreaming or methodical activity back-firing is what the viewer is relating to.

Critique

When critiquing movement theater pieces (your own or anyone else's) there are several essentials to consider:

1 What happened (the nutshell version)
2 Impact
3 Performance
4 Structure.

> 1 *What happened in the piece?* Tell us the nutshell synopsis of what you saw. In a linear movement theater construction, it is important that the audience follow the storyline. In an abstract work, it is important that they are left with the intended emotion. It is useful to have an outside eye— what was conveyed may be very different than what was intended, and the point of art, after all, is communication.

2   *Did the work have an impact on you?* Was it satisfying? How? Was there anything that was particularly compelling? What? If the piece was playful fluff, was it entertaining? And if it was abstract in nature, did the movement resonate and leave you with an emotion?

3   *Comment on the performance.* Was it well-executed? Were the techniques precise and well-paced? Were the performers believable?

4   *Comment on the structure.* Was there a beginning and middle and an end? (Even the most abstract work needs to have an introduction, climax, and resolution.) Were the devices or techniques that were used effective in conveying the desired result? What worked and what did not? If there was music, did it support the intention of the piece? If there were props or costumes, did they contribute something significant or were they just icing on the cake?

You will find that the most compelling work stems from someplace personal. Honestly mining your own experiences can deliver universal truths.

Scenario 3: getting over Bruce

A woman sits alone onstage reading a letter. A man behind her on the diagonal gestures "stop," "finished," "list of reasons" in a personal vocabulary of hieroglyphics. This repeats several times with different rhythms and emphasis of gesture. She is immobile.

She puts the letter purposefully on the ground and sits slowly back to face the audience as the man walks across stage stopping behind her chair.

He repeats the same signals, but this time violently, using his entire body to create the signals, and with each action she reacts with an equally violent response, contracted inward on the chair and conversely thrown open arms and legs splayed out. They never touch each other, or acknowledge each other's presence.

This "attack" ends with them both abruptly turning profile away from each other and nostalgic dance music begins playing (perhaps 1940s big band), and a couple enter upstage and begin a long sensual dance, responding intimately to gestures and movements of the other.

This scenario is the tantalizing introduction to a larger movement theater piece. Immobility and then causality and repetition drive the dramatic action, effectively initiating us into this broken romance. Abstract movement theater construction benefits from compositional exercises. This scenario is your bridge to structuring group action in space for optimum dramatic impact.

Structural thoughts for group movement: floor pattern

Choreographer Lucinda Childs worked for many years using geometric floor patterns as a primary structural element of her dances. Using a simple vocabulary of motion (a jump, walking, running) on a clear grid in space, her work was geometric, meditative, and engaging. Below are some structural ways of organizing floor pattern.

Spatial orientation If four people are walking in single file across the room, and they simultaneously turn and walk toward us, they have broken our expectations. They have gone from a sequential line in space to a mass motion forward. This is a simple dramatic use of floor pattern. Marching bands are an example of floor pattern in unison movement. The organized geometry of the grid can be comforting, intellectually intriguing, and as unexpected as a turn of the kaleidoscope. The elements are the same, but with a slight twist of orientation, the picture is entirely different.

Unison movement Simultaneity of action implies agreement, and well-executed unison motion allows the audience to relax, secure in the implied harmony. Broken unison is dramatic; you "break" the implied status quo. Sudden unison out of individual movements is also dramatically effective. The world you thought was fragmented is really whole.

Split screen: juxtaposition Performers placed on a diagonal in space are perceived as individual entities, and yet there is an implied relationship evoked by their simultaneous presence. If they execute unison movement simultaneously, we perceive commonality. If one begins the movement phrase and the second follows, we still perceive commonality, but with a power structure of initiator and follower. If they execute two different types of movement (perhaps the performer in the back is continuously repeating one action, while the performer in the front executes a combination of different movement phrases), we still see a connection, but a connection that requires more information before digesting it. However, because of the repetition of the movement in the back, we can accept the changing actions in the front and not feel that we have missed out on something.

As we've mentioned earlier, if two performers enact two different combinations of changing action, the audience's eye cannot process the cluttered information and the impact is lessened. Causality is, once again, a powerful ally so use the split screen wisely to support your point.

Choreography experiments

These exercises should be done without thought or stopping so that each new command leads to complicit unison action that seamlessly flows out of the previous action. Repeat a movement for as long as it takes for the group to perform it accurately and in unison. Then it will be time for the next command. Work with music (style of your choosing) with a steady beat. As dancers know, music codifies rhythmic counts, making your movement consistent and easier to repeat. These exercises are presented for a group of nine actors, but most can be adapted for a smaller number and all can be adapted for a much larger group.

Trio vocabulary exercise

Start milling with the group (reminding yourself to keep a consistent pace and focus as you make effortless adjustments and interactions).

Move into backward milling, and after establishing a comfortable flow of energy within the group while moving backward, return to forward milling.

Move seamlessly out of the milling, into trios moving together through space. Allow a leader to emerge, who will initiate your trio action and notice that your normal milling activity (walking) is now slightly more stylized. You are now no longer simply milling, but moving in unison in the walking "style" established by this new leader. Each leader will unconsciously impose a style that organically develops out of their way of walking. Be conscious of it, and play with it. Change leaders two more times, effortlessly adapting to the new walking variations.

Repeat the final unison variation until everyone is uniform in execution. This final movement variation will be the vocabulary for your trio in the next exercise.

Composition exercise 1

Exaggerate or "embroider" this motion so that it becomes bigger and more defined (for example, a normal skipping motion might become an exaggerated jump in the air propelled by arms swinging overhead). Make sure that the action is repeatable. Anyone in the trio can initiate a change—you are now working as a democratic group, so decide as a group what the embroidery will be.

Present your unison movement variation or "phrase," repeating it several times.

Watch other trios presenting their movement phrases.

Watch two trios simultaneously presenting their movement phrases side by side.

The viewer inevitably constructs a relationship between these two arbitrarily juxtaposed trios. After all, the great French existentialist philosopher Camus defined art as the desire of man to impose structure on the chaos of existence. We naturally look for meaning in the juxtaposed movements, and we can use this search for meaning to note similarities and differences in rhythm, locomotion, and use of shape between the two groups. And then note what combinations of these qualities are pleasing.

Show all of the trios in different combinations, and discuss successful combinations.

Remember that there are no absolutes here. Aesthetics are personal, and your enjoyment of a trio hopping in consistent rhythm juxtaposed to a trio executing slow-motion lunges is worthy of comment. It is also worthy to note what intention the audience gleans from the juxtapostion (does it feel like the playful "hoppers" are a commentary on the slower and perhaps more determined "lungers?"). Whatever the response, file it away in your mind for future choreographic reference—we can only learn what is effective for the audience by experimenting, discussing, and then hording the visceral memory for future use.

Composition exercise 2 (using eight counts)

Compose a solo movement phrase connected to an emotion (for example, reaching and releasing).

Embroider that motion. (Reaching might swing up with an extended leg as well as an arm, and releasing might entail a half-turn away, combining momentum and intention.)

Find what organically comes next. (For instance, the half-turn release might continue the momentum of turning away into a full spin that ends with arms wrapped around the body.) You have eight counts to fill with sequential organic phrases. Repeat your entire movement sequence or "combination" of phrases until it feels consistent and countable.

Show your movement combination, and look at the other combinations.

Split into three groups. Choose three of these combinations, and have the three "creators" teach their composition to the group. (One combination to each group: choose combinations that are easy to execute for the individuals involved.)

Watch all three groups executing their combination in perfect unison.

Questions come up when you prepare to show group movement. How far apart should the performers stand? And in what pattern: in single file, a triangle, or some other position? After placement of bodies in relationship to each other in space, other intrinsic structural questions emerge. Does everyone have to start the combination at the same time, or can they add in one by one? If the reaching/releasing phrase can be divided into two parts, can one person reach while the other two release/spin (working in canon with the movement phrase, much like a musical round)?

Go back to your group, and this time create a little theatrical statement playing with the placement and sequencing of your movement combination. What kind of power or intention is conveyed with unison motion as opposed to canon? What about building a sequence so that your first phrase is executed by a trio advancing in a straight line toward the audience. Next a central solo figure advances alone as the other two freeze. The solo figure now freezes as the other two almost catch up and then they all move forward together again, but now in a triangular formation with the soloist in the lead. What is conveyed by turning the group profile and repeating the phrase, or by turning the soloist left, and the other two right, and letting them pass each other before all turning front again. (As you can see we are now manipulating spatial orientation mentioned earlier in this chapter.) Play with these orientations using only your trusty movement combination as vocabulary. You will be amazed at how a single simple sequence can be manipulated to resonate in different ways.

Show your newly minted group composition.

Composition exercise 3

Re-visit your personal solo movement combination, and find a partner.

Teach each other your two combinations, and find ways to combine them. You now have double the vocabulary, and can for example, choose to combine the combinations sequentially or juxtapose them, and of course play with your placement in space. Create an additional movement phrase if you find need, that bridges the two combinations. How can you turn these separately manufactured compositions into a conversation or an eloquent duet statement? Take liberties.

Show all the pairs, and share observations.

As we noted earlier, certain rhythmic combinations sequence or juxtapose better than others. When we see two combinations executed simultaneously, we look for the implied relationship—one inevitably dictates how we "see" the other, commenting on it, or framing it. How do these compositional exercises, oriented to the mechanics of positioning bodies in space, contribute to movement theater creation?

Scenario 3: getting over Bruce (continued)

Nostalgic big band music plays and a couple enter upstage and begin a long and sensual dance, responding intimately to the gestures and movements of the other. The original couple are still downstage immobile, and facing away from each other.

The "intimate" couple travel across the stage in sixteen lyrical counts.

Half-way across the stage (after eight counts) a second couple enters from the same location executing the same combination.

After four counts, a third couple enters and begins the combination.

There is a pause, and all upstage couples simultaneously turn front and move downstage toward the audience in the same lyrical steps, but this time they are all separate individuals executing the movement. This will take sixteen counts.

In the same sixteen counts, the immobile man slowly turns to face the audience and slashes the air with a sharp percussive gesture. The immobile woman responds immediately afterwards in a sharp contraction. Every four counts there is a percussive "hit" with corresponding violent contraction or extension.

One by one the women in the intimate couples respond with the downstage woman, and remain immobile in place afterwards. The men progress downstage until the end of the sixteen counts.

Pause.

The original couple turn to face each other and, grabbing wrists, execute a series of counterbalanced lifts and falls while the others watch. This duet culminates in the woman reaching for the letter.

When she touches the letter, the watching women and men simultaneously turn profile in opposite directions and run forward for four steps and then back for three steps, the ebb and flow of opposing waves of motion. This is repeated a few more times with increasing urgency until all of the couples have exited leaving the original couple alone on stage.

They have never stopped moving, and are gesticulating to each other in a private hieroglyphics, changing positions with each gestural sequence. Sometimes the man is sitting in the chair or turning it upside down; sometimes the woman is standing on the upside down chair, until finally they are both lying side by side on the ground, adamantly waving their arms in unseen gestures in the air. The arms find each other, and pull them into a mutual embrace.

The resolution of "Getting over Bruce" is up in the air.

The point of the exercise is to follow the creative line of thought and play from concept to physicalization. The basic theme and conflict was established beforehand, each moment was developed using compositional techniques tempered by a strong dramatic through-line and an active imagination. The creative physical actor brings a personal sense of integrity to movement theater creation and uses all the tools at his/her fingertips to communicate.

You can finish the scenario.

Index